Old Ystrad Mynach

including

Hengoed, Cefn Hengoed and Maesycwmmer

in Photographs

by Maldwyn Griffiths and Richard Herold

Foreword by
Mervyn Burtch M.B.E.

Volume 2

Old Bakehouse Publications

Abertillery

First published in September 2004

ISBN 1 874538 33 6

Published in the U.K. by
Old Bakehouse Publications
Church Street,
Abertillery, Gwent NP13 1EA
Telephone: 01495 212600 Fax: 01495 216222
Email: oldbakehouseprint.co.uk

Made and printed in the UK
by J.R. Davies (Printers) Ltd.

Foreword

by
Mervyn Burtch MBE

In a recent newspaper article I came across a very telling sentence which ran as follows:- *'We cannot apprehend who we are now if we cultivate ignorance of how we were then'*.

The sentiment seems to encapsulate the aim of books such as this present volume which strive to illuminate our lives by showing what our recent history has been. Just as, genetically speaking, we are governed by the same biological make up as our ancestors, so our way of life has been moulded by many generations of people who have lived and worked in our local communities.

The argument may well be put forward by some misguided individuals that, in an age of globalisation and instant 'celebrity' status (often built on very brittle foundations), the local and the particular are of little value. But this is not so.

The day to day working and thinking of a community is the bedrock on which such a community and ultimately a nation, is based. The historical perspective which books like this gives us, enriches our lives because it helps us to understand our own heritage. There is a grave danger that with current values, what we see on that little oblong box in the corner of the room will seem more real than our own lives. It will be a sad day if virtual reality takes over from reality itself.

When Alexander Pope wrote *'The proper study of mankind is man'*, he was thinking of a broad canvas but his statement applies equally to our own local interests, and to understand the society in which we live, we need to know how it arrived at its present state. When Dr. Johnson wrote *'he who is tired of London is tired of life'*, he was expressing one person's fascination with the life around him.

It is true that *'he who is tired of Ystrad Mynach is tired of life'* does not have quite the same ring, but it expresses a universal truth. What goes on from day to day in our own local communities is endlessly fascinating and important.

Enjoy this book!

Contents

Introduction

We have a lot to thank the people for, that began to take an interest in sport during the 1920s and helped to create some of the sports teams in the Rhymney Valley, competing and winning the best in South Wales. Ystrad Mynach Bowls Club celebrated its 75th anniversary in 2002 and in that period has produced a collection of outstanding teams, pairs and individuals. Penallta Rugby Club, which celebrated its 50th anniversary in 2002, were winners of the Welsh District Cup in 2001, playing at the Millennium Stadium, Cardiff and in the same year were winners of the Rhondda and East Glamorgan League. Other notable anniversaries of long-standing local organisations include the Boys Club which was formed in an old tin shed in Lewis Street in 1933 and still survives today and now of course, the girls are most welcome. Ystrad Mynach Library recently marked its 30th birthday with an open-day and a specially-made decorative cake for the event in the shape of a tier of books!

Whilst a number of these organizations have endured the years, some have not been quite so fortunate. The number of churches and chapels for instance has been dwindling constantly through lack of support, most recently Tabor Chapel in Maesycwmmer and Tabernacle in Raglan Road, Hengoed closed their doors for the last time. On the business front, Gwynn's Garage which closed in the late 1990s, was almost a landmark in the area, having traded for some eighty years with the distinction of selling the very first motor cars in the valley. That Victorian piece of architecture, the viaduct, and probably the largest of local landmarks still stands as a reminder of a century of rail travel that once was and now plays the part of a popular cycle track and pleasant walkway.

Local residents of all the areas covered in this book have been most helpful in a number of ways. Some of the more mature members have been busy relating their memories of years gone by, many of which have now been collated and donated to Ystrad Mynach Library for posterity. Such tales as the mountain fighters of Maesycwmmer and as Mrs. Phyllis Davies recalled, the day when herding some cows and bulls from Ystrad to their farm in Park Road, Hengoed, the inevitable happened; a bull breaking loose, charged its way into the doorway of a former sweet shop on King's Hill and seemed extremely interested in the confectionery on offer whilst a terrified shopkeeper could do no more than look on. Nancy and Marion Gurner have recalled when as little girls they were give all sorts of explanations as to how babies arrived in the world; there was utter amazement that a nurse would pay a visit to the household carrying a small black bag and leave behind a new addition to the family crying its eyes out. These stories of course are without end and all help to paint a picture of local history of which we should all be very proud. The lower part of the Rhymney Valley has of course always been a favourite holiday destination and the following cartoon, kindly donated to the library by the master of such humour, Grenfell Jones M.B.E., further promotes a welcome to the hillsides that surround us.

" LOOK, WE DON'T CARE WHAT IT COSTS US, BUT CAN YOU MANAGE TO GET US SOMETHING IN EITHER HENGOED, MAESYCWMMER OR YSTRAD MYNACH?"

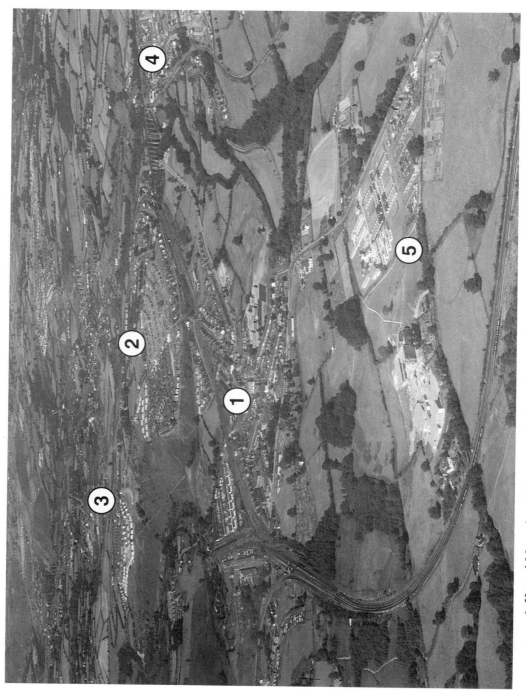

1. Ystrad Mynach, 2. Hengoed, 3. Cefn Hengoed, 4. Maesycwmmer, 5. Lower Ystrad Mynach.

CHAPTER 1

Ystrad Mynach

1. The familiar cloth cap can be seen worn by these gentlemen in this 1920s photograph that was taken on the corner of the Beech Square in Ystrad Mynach. There was little fear of being knocked down by speeding traffic in those days as they pose by the signpost showing Nelson to be two miles distant. At the time this photograph was taken, Gwynn's garage sold the first motor car in the area.

2. The Beech Square or 'The Shant' as it was once called can be seen here on a cold autumn morning in 1954 and the familiar sight of the local painter and decorator's motor-bike and sidecar belonging to Mr. James Lessimore can be seen to the right of the picture. The Palace Cinema is on the left and at the time filmgoers would be watching two films in an evening classed as an A and a supporting B film showing Monday to Wednesday. A new programme would be shown Thursday to Saturday and a separate one on Sunday, such was the popularity of the cinema. The film showing at the time of this photograph was '20,000 Leagues Under The Sea' starring Kirk Douglas and James Mason.

3. A 1960s view looking towards the Beech Tree Hotel taken when traffic congestion was not a problem. In between the parked cars to the right of the picture can be seen the familiar sight of Tim Waters' butcher's bicycle and he recalls pedalling this heavy bike with no gears, up and down the villages. It could well have been good training for the Tour De France but he decided to carry on the Waters name in the butchery trade, proud of the fact that they are one of the oldest established traders.

4. Looking down a thriving Penallta Road towards the Pierhead building during the 1960s. Many people will recall some of the main shops on this part of the road which included Boots the chemist on the right hand side, not forgetting the Co-op butchery and grocery departments, Shakespeare the jewellers and Massari's Café which is still trading today. On the left there was for many years Mathews the builders merchants.

5. Penallta Road can be seen here in the early 1960s before the ground on the left was built upon. Ashburne Fabricare now occupies much of this particular spot, being well-known for their dry-cleaning, home valet service and extensive range of Welsh products; owners Gerrard and Meryl Lewis are proud of their graceful shop-fronts and Welsh window display. The Viceroy of India Balti Restaurant and Job Centre also occupy part of this area.

6. The staff of the butchers and drapery departments of the Ystrad Mynach branch of the Co-operative Society, Penallta Road, pose for this 1921 photograph. In the picture are Ted Lewis, unknown, Mr. Lewis, Mr. Richards (Treharris), Harold George, Mr. Maddox, Mr. Evans, Mr. Ivor Webb, Mr. Lloyd, Edith Truman, Elsie Baker, Nancy Harding, Doris Kedwood, Mrs. Williams, Mr. Powell and Mr. Carpenter.

7. A very quiet morning on Bedwlwyn Road when this photograph was taken in the 1940s. Some of the shops at this time would have been Oliver's shoes, Williams the dentist, Maddox the butcher, Star grocery and Hughes drapery.

8./9. Two views of Commercial Street taken from the same spot some 60 years apart. The scene above is prior to the building of the distinctive Pierhead and a horse and carriage, possibly belonging Colonel Lindsay can be seen outside the town's gents' clothing shop. The lower picture from around the 1960s, shows the same shop still trading as a men's outfitters and called the Bon owned by Mr. Perkins. This particular shop still trades as a gents' outfitters a century on and is currently owned by Mr. Lyn Tudor.

10. The open fields of lower Ystrad Mynach during the late 1950s saw the development of the College, Graddfa School and the building of Troedyrhiw estate. The view here is of the first steps which in technical terms would be, commence reduce dig in preparation for concrete and reinforced foundations of the College. The unspoilt view of Troedyrhiw Farm can be seen at the top of the picture.

11. The Coopers Arms is situated in the lower part of Ystrad Mynach and this photograph was taken in 1908, the owners at the time being Mr. Daniel Thomas and his wife Ann who brewed their own beer here until they sold the business in 1913. Also in the picture are Miss Rachel Thomas and miners from Llanbradach and Penallta collieries. The Coopers was allowed to open at 6.30 in the morning for the benefit for workers from the mines after finishing their night shift.

12. The scene here is of Edward Street at the lower end of Ystrad Mynach amidst decorations in celebration of the Coronation in 1953. The huts to be seen at the end of the street were built as accommodation for so-called 'Bevin Boys' - workers who due to acute labour shortages, were directed to work in the coal mines instead of military conscription during the Second World War.

13. A charming country scene is shown here of the mill and forge on the old Caerphilly Road at lower Ystrad Mynach. Although the mill is no longer in use, Mr. John West the forge owner and blacksmith, can be proud of the exceptionally high standard of work produced at the forge and in maintaining the building's tradition. The house adjoining the 400 year-old forge was the first known post office in the area.

14./15. These two photographs are exceptionally rare and anyone looking at them would find it hard to believe that they were of the Royal Oak in Ystrad Mynach at the turn of the 20th century. The top photograph shows the front with the owners Mr. and Mrs. Williams who were landlords whilst the lower photograph shows the side of the building. Mr. Williams is seen looking on as the drayman who has just restocked the pub's finest beer, pushes the empty barrel up the slight gradient.

16./17. The two pictures here are taken from nearly the same spot some 60 years apart. The Royal Oak was originally a much smaller building as seen above, but was virtually knocked down and completely rebuilt in 1912 into one of the finest buildings in the valley. The pub's landlords have included Mr. Williams from around the turn of the century until 1926, Mr. Harry Green 1926 to 1947, Mr. and Mrs. Richardson and their daughter Patricia 1947 to 1963, Bernard and Patricia Murphy 1963 to 1991 and Roger and Lucy Wood from 1991 until the present day.

18. Bedlwyn Road taken around 1910 at a time when the town was beginning to expand rapidly. The pine end of the building to the left of the picture shows that the lower half of the road has not yet been built. This was completed in 1912 when the Arcade and Pierhead was finished by local builder Mr. Jones.

19. Bedwlwyn Road Ystrad Mynach at the turn of the century or Pontargylla as it was then known. The only mode of transport is the horse and cart with a lone pedestrian standing in front of Pontargylla Cottage. Panteg Cottages can be seen to the bottom right which at the time were owned by William and Margaret James and for a period, this was the site of the main bank in the town.

20. Flooding had always been a problem in this part of Ystrad Mynach prior to much needed improvements to combat the rising water of the Rhymney River. Mr Derek Packer braved the swell to take this photograph in the 1960s of what is now called the New Cottage Dance Centre. Fortunately the work done has prevented any further troubles with the river.

21. Penalltau Isaf Farm, situated just above Ystrad Mynach and just below the site of Penallta Colliery is seen here during the early years of the 20th century. It was the birthplace of Dr. Thomas Llewellyn, a leading supporter of Welsh language religious publishing. He is mostly remembered for his campaign to publish Welsh Bibles and by 1769 more than 20,000 had been printed, thanks to many donations and his own generosity.

22. A view of Brynmynach Avenue taken in the 1940s and looking towards Penallta rocks. Tredomen works and the NCB offices were just to the left at the end of the Avenue and Brynmynach Farm just visible on the right of the picture, now exists as the centre of a housing complex.

23. Mrs. Margaret Davies is seen here as she looks towards the stunning rock formation of Ystrad Mynach, rocks that are at the end of Brynmynach Avenue in the picture above. The Vale of Neath railway line is just in view as it runs besides the rocks, they providing a big attraction to passengers travelling along this route.

24. London House Ystrad Mynach was owned by Mr. and Mrs. E.H. Williams and was one of the finest shops in the village and the surrounding area for over 60 years. It had a variety of departments that included Hosiery, Millinery, Carpets, Mantles, Linoleum, Dresses and some of the finest lace around.

25. Gwynn's was a well-known garage in the valleys, it being founded in 1918 and the first car retailer in the area. It was a sad end when the garage closed in the late 1990s after nearly 80 years of service, with garages and petrol pumps in Ystrad and at the viaduct in Hengoed. The Institute dance hall stands close by and was renowned during the 1950s and '60s for the rock 'n roll and beat groups that appeared there. It was also noted for being the first to have maple flooring installed, a 'must' for dancing lovers everywhere. The Institute was built in the 1920s under the auspices of the Miners Welfare Fund.

CHAPTER 2

Hengoed

26. Hengoed Post Office, Raglan Road in about 1905. Although the post office was in Hengoed it was originally called Maesycwmmer Post Office, partly due to the growth of industry and housing in Maesycwmmer as most of Hengoed at this time had already been developed.

27. This view overlooking Hengoed taken from Maesycwmmer some forty years ago, shows open fields where since have appeared the Avenue, a Tesco supermarket and the Ystrad Mynach by-pass. Above these open fields ran the Rhymney Valley and Neath to Pontypool railway lines together with Park Road and what were called the red houses built in the 1950s. Hengoed Institute can be seen at the top of the picture, a building that was demolished in the 1970s due to land subsidence and to the left, part of Graig houses is to be seen.

28. An impressive view of the Graig in Hengoed as viewed from Ystrad Mynach in 1921. The railway line that ran just below has long been replaced by a cycle track. To the right of the picture is Bedwlwyn farm, another feature that has since disappeared; it was here that great concern was felt in the 1930s when a case of what is today known as 'mad cow's disease' was reported for the first time.

29./30. The Cross Keys in Cefn Hengoed is a fine architectural building that stands on the brow of the village which can be seen for many miles, and from the function room there is a commanding view of the village that was built for workers of Penallta Colliery. A wheelbarrow race was one of the pub's events as can be seen below during the early 1960s, with Ronnie Carroll and Trevor Bower (Digger). Two locals John Wilding and Dai Brooks are two of the onlookers.

31. The area of Hengoed shown here is just north of the viaduct and was taken in approximately 1905. The white building in the centre has just been built as is that of the post office in Raglan Road. This picture postcard gives the viewer another chance to see Hills Terrace and the cottages at the bottom of King's Hill that no longer exist.

32. An impressive view of the viaduct that is impossible to see nowadays due the concrete works and the extensive growth of trees. A lone figure standing next to the tree on the left helps illustrate the sheer scale of viaduct with its 16 arches. The woollen mill of Maesycwmmer is seen standing just below and to the right of the viaduct.

33. The lower part of King's Hill during the 1960s when it was a thriving little complex of shops. Hengoed station is to the top left and just in view is the Junction Inn that has the well-known sign of two trains passing over each other on the Neath to Pontypool and Rhymney railway lines.

34. A 1950s photograph taken of the area near the viaduct and one that some local inhabitants may easily recall, but difficult for many, due to the changes that have since taken place. Hill's Terrace and Club Row are on the left and on the right is Gwynn's Garage that was additional to their sales and servicing in Ystrad. As can be seen, these were quieter and safer days and crossing the road here was an easy task compared to today with the volume of traffic that now passes this way.

35. A 1940s view of Alexandra Road, Hengoed, with two ladies taking a well deserved break after just completing a part of their daily chores that was much a part of their everyday life. They would take great pride in these chores which involved regular sweeping and scrubbing of the pavement and door step, the brass letter box would always be gleaming bright. There was very little rubbish for the refuse-collector as most things would be burned on the open coal fire with only ashes remaining as can be seen to the right on the road that has not been properly surfaced.

36. The development of Raglan Road is well underway with this view that was taken from a few yards from the post office on the right. Hengoed Tabernacle, built in 1906, can be seen looking considerably closer than it is. Gittens and Hayter Limited, a long-established engineering company now occupies this space.

37. A birds eye view of Kings Hill Hengoed. The Hengoed County Girls School is seen on the right of this photograph with the caretaker's lodge at the junction of Alexandra Road in the centre of this 1918 scene.

38. Hengoed County Girls School can be seen here showing its superb architectural features, a fine building that unfortunately fell victim to surrounding land subsidence and had to be pulled down. Girls intent on furthering their education at this highly reputable school were known to have travelled from places such as Trelewis and Bedlinog, journeys often taking up to an hour and a half in each direction by bus and train.

39./40. Two views of Hengoed High Level station on the Neath to Pontypool line. The first view is looking towards Park Road in busier days with a Pontypool-bound train approaching the platform whilst below, the scene is a sorry sight looking towards the viaduct in the 1960s after the closure of the line and start of dismantling. Passengers on this route would enjoy scenes of outstanding beauty as they travelled over the viaduct and for all who remember the age of steam, there was nothing to rival the sight, sounds and smell of a train with its smoke bellowing away.

41. A very quiet morning in Brynavon Terrace is evident here some fifty years ago with the Coronation Store's morning delivery taking place on the right. Mrs. Thomas can be seen in the window above, what was at one time Gittens the builder's office. The Ford van facing the camera belonged to Evans Stores which is first right in the photograph and some readers may also remember Mr. Williams who owned the newsagents opposite this store at the time.

42. This one hundred-year-old photograph of Park Road shows it to contain houses of some extravagance for the period, full of Victorian and Edwardian character. There were clear views of the hillside of Maesycwmmer and more unspoilt scenery down the valley towards Caerphilly and its mountainside. The only blot on the landscape might have been the close proximity of a busy railway line, a mixture of convenience for the traveller and smoke and noise for the inhabitants.

43. An aerial view of the NCB houses in Hengoed that was taken during the 1990s and it shows the new road at the top of the picture. Hengoed Baptist Chapel that was founded in 1650 can be seen in the foreground of the picture.

CHAPTER 3

Maesycwmmer

44. The view here is looking towards Thomas Street and the old bridge in Maesycwmmer, taken from Hengoed High level station in the early 1960s. A van can be seen making its way towards the village around the series of sharp bends and the old bridge carrying the Newport to Brecon railway was a nightmare for the wool-laden lorries from the nearby mill. Just like many other older buildings, Thomas Street which ran alongside the railway line and the bridge has long gone.

45. The scene here of a march is believed to be a celebration of peace to mark the end of World War One in November 1918. The procession is made up of children with some wonderful costumes with Santa Claus as the main symbol of peace and is seen passing the Angel Inn with a clear view over the roof tops of Thomas Street, the Butchers Arms and arches of the viaduct.

46. The shops in Commercial Street, Maesycwmmer are seen here in 1910, once a thriving part of the village, they growing in number as the industrial revolution progressed in the area. Railways, small mines, levels, the chemical and brick works all played their part in providing plenty of jobs and population expansion and yet nowadays Maesycwmmer is just a shadow of its former self.

47./48. The Maesycwmmer Inn is seen here during the 1960s before the pub was extended. Landlords Dennis and Molly Barwood are seen here ready to welcome you with drink and hot and cold snacks that were available in the bar. The once-familiar sign of the Rhymney Brewery sign can be seen in the top picture, their beers being sold across South Wales and claimed by many to be one of the finest beers available.

49. This is how Tabor Road in Maesycwmmer looked back in the 1960s, long before the motor car became the essential part of life that it is today. As local readers will know, it would be impossible to take a similar such photograph these days thanks to the change in lifestyle and rise in the standard of living that has provided a minimum of one vehicle for virtually every household these days.

50. The picturesque scene of Summerfield Hall Lane, Gellihaf Lane and Victory Road is the setting for this photograph taken in September 1927. All Saints Church can be seen to the right of the picture with the Brecon and Merthyr railway lines running just above the church.

51. Many people may recall the old lane running alongside the Butchers Arms leading onto Victoria Road and the old bridge running under the Brecon and Merthyr Railway. The little winding lane ran under the bridge turning and twisting its way under the viaduct and over the Rhymney River and on to Hengoed. Steam pours out of a Brecon-bound train as it waits at Maesycwmmer station before carrying on its journey under the curved arch of the viaduct.

52. The full 16 arches and curve of the viaduct can be seen in this 1950s view taken from Maesycwmmer. Mrs. Herbert's shop can be seen on the left, a shop that was a delight for young children to pay a visit and said to have had the finest toffee apples and selection of home-made sweets in the whole valley. The last scheduled passenger train passed over the viaduct in June 1964.

53. The once thriving main street of Maesycwmmer can be seen here in about 1910 and shows the old road and a collection of shops, long before major road-widening completely transformed the scene. Some of the popular old shops such as Central Stores, Gandertons cycle shop and the Travellers Rest Inn were on the top left, all sorely-missed once modern planning took hold during the 1960s.

54. A further opportunity to see the lower part of Main Street/Commercial Street in 1906 looking upwards to Bank House and the Co-op building. Bank House acquired its name from days when the front room was used for a few hours a week as a branch of the London Provincial Bank whilst one of the other rooms provided a part-time doctor's surgery. Some readers and local inhabitants may also remember the small billiard hall that stood just below Bank House.

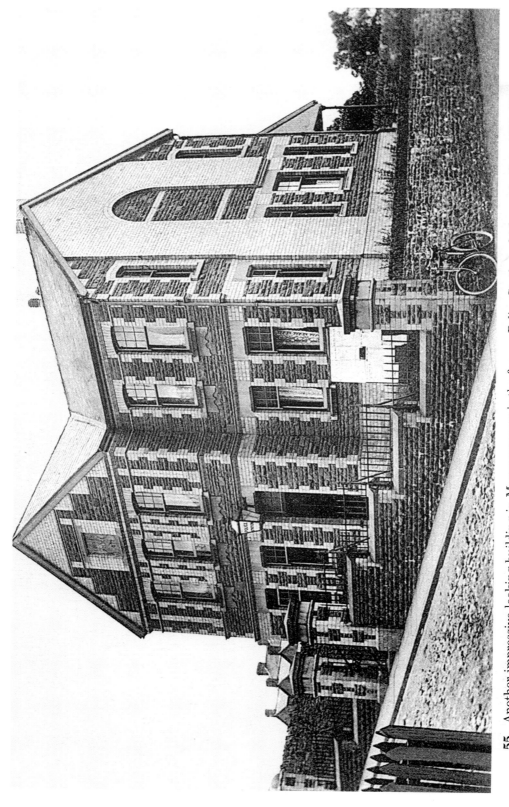

55. Another impressive-looking building in Maesycwmmer is the former Police Station which was built in 1899. This was a more permanent residence, replacing stations that had seen a number of different locations around the village over the years. At the time of this photograph a Mr. O. Lawrence was in charge of law and order in the vicinity.

56. One of the finest views that some could wish to see was that from the windows of a steam-hauled train passing over the viaduct. This picture is almost a hundred years old and shows a train having just left Hengoed High Level station on its way to cross another viaduct at Crumlin en route for Pontypool and Hereford. Through the arches of the viaduct are open fields as they were prior to the building of Raglan Road. The woollen mill at this time was in its hey-day and can be seen just below the viaduct.

57. The organisers and residents of this finely decorated street in Maesycwmmer can be seen here possibly preparing for a lavish party to celebrate the Queen's Silver Jubilee in 1977. This street is somewhat unique, it being blessed with three different names - North Avenue, Chave Terrace and Provident Cottages!

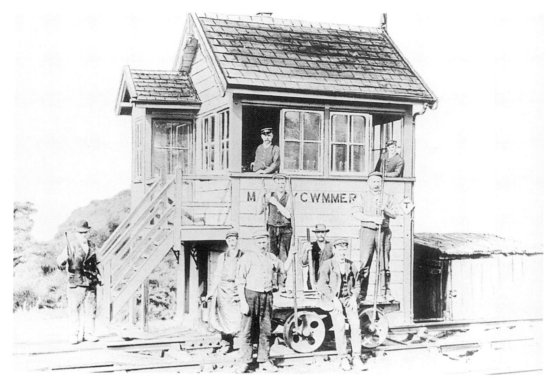

58. A rare photograph of what appears to be the maintenance and railway workers along with signalmen during the early stages of Maesycwmmer railway lines and station.

59. It is forty years since a train passed this way and this particular view may jog the memories of some readers as the tracks are in the process of being taken up and the houses of Thomas Street await their fate. This photograph provides another chance to see the old road that passed the Butchers Arms and wound its way under the railway bridge making its way through the viaduct arches to other side of the Rhymney River.

CHAPTER 4

Industry and Commerce

60. A photograph of what must have been an enjoyable break from school work for these lads from Pengam Grammar School who were treated to a visit to Penallta Colliery by their science master and school photographer Mr. Arthur Wright. The year is 1910 and in the foreground is Number 1 downcast shaft with Number 2 upcast behind; the large building on the left would have been the powerhouse.

61./62. The sinking of Penallta Colliery began with the cutting of the first sod by the wife of Colonel Lindsay in 1905, the actual spade used on the day now being on display at Elliot Winding Museum and kindly loaned by members of the Lindsay family. The two photographs seen here were taken in 1906 by Arthur Wright showing the shaft-sinkers as work gradually progressed to considerable depths. Those depths would eventually reach 2,400 feet and 1,955 feet to pit bottom with a diameter of 21 feet placing them amongst the deepest in the South Wales coalfield. The lower picture shows some of the banksmen at the colliery.

63. The precise date here is recorded as October 14th 1906 with Penallta in its early working days under the ownership of the Powell Duffryn Steam Coal Company, which by 1910 had turned it into one of their most successful collieries, exporting coal around the world. Close examination of Number 1 downcast shaft will reveal a man working at the top and the boilerhouse chimney has been constructed with a temporary corrugated building just behind the shaft.

64. Photographs of some relics from Penallta's past including pit-checks and baths and canteen tickets that were kindly loaned by mining enthusiast Mr. Hywell Roberts who with his vast collection of mining memorabilia caused great interest when appearing on television.

65. The staff of Ystrad Mynach Library accompanied by star attraction Mr. Mervyn Burtch holding his recently-awarded M.B.E. This important valley library having celebrated thirty years of service to the community by holding an open-day, now offers the availability of the latest computer technology and internet access in addition to a wide variety of reading material.

66. An important function during the 1939-45 War was constant vigilance in the wake of enemy attack and such bodies as the Auxiliary Fire Service and Police Specials were established to play their part. Seen here is a group of Police with their superintendent photographed at the back of the Ystrad Mynach Police Station and one of their duties would have been keeping an eye on the viaduct which at the time was seen as an easy target for the Luftwaffe or saboteurs. The Police Specials were made up mainly of village businessmen that included in the back row Mr. Emlyn Lloyd the ironmonger, Mr. Robinson the chemist and John Mallon. In the middle row Mr. Guppy the butcher, Mr. Evan Richards the undertaker and builder, Mr. Trevor Davies and Mr. Arthur Williams.

67. A view of Tredomen Engineering Works which was built by the Powell Duffryn Steam Coal Company in 1922 for the manufacture and supply of machinery for their numerous collieries, the undertaking being absorbed by the National Coal Board after nationalisation. In its heyday Tredomen provided up to 630 valuable jobs in the area and in this picture, the offices above the workshops were to become the NCB Computer Centre.

68. The former expanse of the works is clearly visible from the air, it occupying a site of more than 16 acres at one stage. The villages of Tredomen and Brynmynach are in the top of the picture with Ystrad Mynach at the top left.

69. The workers here have been allowed a short break for this unique photograph that was taken during the construction of the sizeable Tredomen Works in 1922 on behalf of the also sizeable Powell Duffryn Company.

70. Tredomen Managing Director Mr. William Norman with the works medical team during the 1960s. He recalls starting as an apprentice at the works for the princely sum of 40 pence per week and still retains the original payslip as a gentle reminder. Born in Hengoed, Mr. Norman completed his engineering training during the war years, when the works switched manufacturing over to vital munitions and went on through the ranks of supervision, management to Chief Executive. Many of the technical advances at Tredomen were down to his efforts having studied modern engineering practices within the U.K. and Europe. Also included in this photograph are Stuart Mullins, Sister Jarman, Andy Payne, Alan Edwards, Clive Phillips, Tony Davies and Ron James.

71./72. Two interior views of the works illustrating weapon manufacture there between 1939 and 1945. On the left, machining of a turret for a Churchill tank is in progress whilst below, the foundry is seen with a stockpile of casings for 500 pound bombs. During the war Tredomen was seconded to produce many other articles of weaponry such as gun barrels, breech blocks, boat anchors for the Ministry of Aircraft Production and Admiralty. The site was renowned for its rate of productivity of such components and was considered to have been most fortunate in never to have been the victim of enemy attack!

73. Messers Harry Holder and Gethin Thomas during their working days at Maesycwmmer Mill, stand upon a well-stacked lorry load of wool during the early 1960s. There are those who will still remember the sight of patient truck drivers making their way around the twisting lane to the mill and negotiating the old bridge. Local folklore has it that parts of the mill were haunted by a restless spirit and of visitors purposely avoiding a second visit to some areas!

74. Local inhabitant Cyril Roberts is seen here demonstrating his skills of riding a nineteenth-century bicycle the 'penny-farthing', so-called due to its design of a huge front wheel and minute rear wheel so-named after the coinage of the day. The saying 'coming a cropper' originates from use of this machine, when leaning just a little too far forward, the rider would be pitched well over the top of the front wheel.

75. A Number 21 Bedford O.W.B. bus on Pengam Road, Ystrad Mynach en route for Bargoed, Brithdir and Ogilvie collieries and it is stood at one of the pick-up points for some of the 'Bevin Boys' employed in the mines at the time. Bert Evans of Glyngaer, a bus driver for thirty years is in the centre of the picture accompanied by conductor Wilf James and a prospective passenger. Long after retirement, the collection of bus memorabilia was still the hobby of Mr. Evans and has now carried on to his son.

76. The proprietors and fitters of Dainton Brothers Garage, situated at the rear of Brynavon Terrace, Hengoed are seen here in 2003, the business having been established since the late 1960s. In the picture are Chris Benbow, Lee Clayton, Leighton Lever, Arthur Dainton (one of the founders), Gareth Dainton, Huw Dainton, Winston Dainton and Gavin Jenkins.

77. The red insignia of the Mobil company above this well-established garage in Cefn Hengoed has been a landmark for many years. When Howard Whittle left the Forces he started a car-hire business in the village for the use of visiting midwives, later securing contracts with Penallta Colliery and local schools. Original vehicles included a seven-seated Bedford with Daimler and Vauxhall cars, familiar sights to many and set up during the 1950s, the business is still run by the same family. In this photograph are Howard, Dave and Steve Whittle with Jim Miles and Carl Lemmon.

78. Local firm Gittens and Hayter Ltd. are well-known professional engineers, toolmakers and machinists who have given service over many years, with Gittens Builders responsible for the construction of many quality houses in the district. Photographed inside the workshop are Paul Hayter in the back with, left to right - Barrie Richards, Leslie Walters, Jamie Hayter, Philip Snailham, Colin Taylor, Mervyn Pryce, Jeremy Hayter, Douglas Stokes, Susan Stokes, Mavis Sherwood and Tudor James.

79. This is an Ystrad Mynach shop that has served as a Gents' Outfitters for close on a century and today's owner is Mr. Lyn Tudor. He took over the business in the 1960s from Mr. John Perkins, the shop now being well-known in the valleys for its ability to supply quality clothing for any occasion. Lyn is pictured here with one of his assistants Kevin Evans.

80. There is a wealth of talent in the area covered by this book and the talent of professional artist Chris Griffin is respected far and wide. He is seen here accompanied by Welsh rugby legend Ieuan Evans who opened an exhibition of Chris's work at the Rhondda Heritage Park, a display that spanned 40 years of the artist's mastery of brush and pen.

81. Were it not for the charitable efforts of numerous organisations in the district, many an institution would be that much poorer and seen here are members of Bargoed's Inner Wheel Club, having presented a chair to Ystrad Mynach Hospital, paid for by one of their many fund-raising events. In amongst the familiar faces are Peggy Gardener, Glenys Tucker, Mary Burgess, Ceridwen Richards, Llewela Richards, Heulwen Mason, Olwen Heenan, Ruth Davies, Audrey Packer and Betty Hood.

82./83. Ystrad Mynach Hospital serves the communities of the town itself and the surrounding areas within the Caerphilly Borough and above is a former Matron, a highly-respected position that has since disappeared in the names of modernisation and rationalisation. The hospital consists of three general wards with 64 beds, dedicated to programmes of rehabilitation, particularly for the more mature adult; the services provided being quite extensive, ranging from Therapies, Stroke Rehabilitation and Palliative Care. As always, voluntary work by the WRVS and League of Friends is a much-appreciated support by this hospital. The photograph below shows the main entrance during the 1950s when it was a long-stay unit.

84./85. An important part of patient care is the nourishment that can be provided and here are two photographs from the hospital's catering department. Above is the serving and trolley area back in the 1950s whilst below, is the scene as it appeared in the year 2003. In this picture are Snr. Nurse David Timmins, Sister Linda Lewis with Myrtle Davies, Kath Smith, Elaine Davies, Siân Clabby, Gaynor Smith, Kath Powell and Helen Hatter.

86. Richard Evans's outfitters shop in 1913 in days when it was customary to display as many goods outside as well as inside. On the left is Mr. Williams, on the right is Leila Edwards and in the centre Nancy (Harding) Gurner a 14 year-old apprentice. In those days most shop-workers needed an apprenticeship of two years without payment! Having completed her training, this lady went on to work at the Co-op Store in Penallta Road, working there until marrying Ernest Gurner; another quite common custom at the time of course was that ladies would be dismissed from their job upon marriage! The Gurner's daughters Nancy Sparham and Marion Davies still reside in the area.

87. An aged view of Maesycwmmer looking down the road towards Ystrad Mynach that shows a fine building of the period. This was part of a complex of shops in Commercial Street or Main Street as it was then known, the Co-op occupying the site for many years and later the Democratic Club which was destroyed by fire during the early 1950s.

88. The Pierhead building at Ystrad Mynach was built in 1912 and very similar in design to that built a year or two earlier in nearby Bargoed. Ystrad's Co-op had their extensive shop here, a shop that sold everything from the world of ladies and gent's fashion, groceries, shoes and even music.

89. This is the grocery department with Mrs. Olwen Hughes stood third from the right. This was long before the arrival of supermarkets, pre-packed food and electronic pricing; these were the days of such things as butter and cheese being in large slabs waiting to be cut to size, weighed accordingly and the eventual bill being handwritten and checked diligently while the customer sat patiently on a chair in front of the counter, all part of a forgotten service these days.

90. Staff and members of the public pose on the platform of Hengoed Station with stationmaster Mr. Harris, Alfred Williams head linesman and William Thomas. The G.W.R. poster is advertising a special concessionary rail trip to Cardiff to watch the fight between Welsh boxing hero Tommy Farr and Frank Moody on August 14th 1935, a match incidentally that ended in a draw. (The re-match took place the following December with Farr winning by a knockout in Round 4).

91. After four and a half years of war, celebrations of peace and gratitude to the fallen of Ystrad Mynach, Hengoed and Garden Village (Cefn Hengoed) were held at Ystrad Fawr on 19th and 21st July 1919, the grounds being kindly loaned by Colonel and Mrs. Lindsay with the roasting of an ox as the centre of attraction. The programme read - *'The Ox which has been supplied by local butchers will be roasted continuously from 12.00 a.m. until 7.00 p.m. and will be distributed free of charge to 1. War Widows and Dependents. 2. Disabled Soldiers, Sailors and their Dependents. 3. Old Age Pensioners. 4. Any Deserving Poor. 5. To the General Public'.*

92./93. Two photographs that were taken a hundred years apart in Commercial Street Maesycwmmer. Originally a greengrocer's and general store it has now been firmly established as the village butchers serving local customers for many years under the ownership of Mr. Brian Crane.

94. Pictured behind the counter of the Central Café in Ystrad Mynach is Lena Massari, now the longest-serving businesswoman in the valley, having started work at the café on September 3rd 1939. Born in the Rhondda Valley in 1920, she still recalls the bloodied faces of her father and brothers following a conflict with the troops that were sent to quell the striking miners of 1926. Her dedication to work was rewarded with a plaque and certificate presented by the Ministry.

95. This is Mr. Arthur Wright, best known for his roles as Chemistry Master, Pengam Boys' School, his work as photographer and author of The History of Lewis School and Church Bells of Monmouth. Having settled in Wales from Norfolk, he was awarded the M.B.E. in 1947 for his services to National Savings, a vital task during the war years in particular. A skilled and enthusiastic photographer, he is seen here equipped and ready for an outing and many of the old postcards and photographs that are available of the local area can be attributed to this gentleman.

96. Just one of the chores endured by this local lady of Ystrad Mynach was doing the family washing. This particular duty was a thankless task, more often than not having to be performed outside and can only be imagined by today's generation. Before the arrival of luxurious washing machines and spin dryers, the ladies' tools of the trade included a large saucepan for boiling water on an open coal fire, large sink bath or tub, large bars of carbolic soap, a scrubbing board, a mangle, a clothes-horse or an airing rack that dangled from the ceiling and a never-ending supply of elbow grease. The latter was probably the most essential, bearing in mind that nearly every household had someone that worked in the local collieries with all the filth they produced. The late Mrs. Cissy Oliver a former teacher of Hengoed and who may be remembered by the more mature residents was one of those ladies who forever refused to move with the times, sticking with her traditional sink and mangle forever and a day.

97. Some local pensioners take the time here to be photographed during a revival of the washerwoman's day and her pieces of equipment and for the younger reader, the lady in the centre operates a 'mangle' - a device for straining the water from the washing before drying and ironing. The next lady shows how to use a scrubbing board and the lady on the right hangs on to a 'clothes horse'.

98. This picture is from around 1914 and shows a workforce of men and women employed in Ystrad Mynach laying one of the first proper Tarmacadam- surfaced roads in the area. One of the plants used for making the tar was situated where the sports hall is now situated and was operated by the Rhymney Valley District Council until the early 1940s. An early machine was a horse-drawn vehicle and villager Mr. Gwyn Jones still recalls one popular animal named 'Pilot', much-loved and fed by the local children of the period.

99. A later picture of some local road workers seen on Bedwas Road at the top of Maesycwmmer during the late 1940s or early 1950s. Some of their names have been traced as Jimmy Hatton, Courtney Green with a young boy John Phillips sat in the wheelbarrow.

100. Mr. David Thomas Meredith who was stationmaster at Maesycwmmer is seen here on the platform outside the booking office during the 1930s, a time when up to fifteen staff were employed at the station and alongside are some reminders of the railway days. Up until the early 1940s, passengers often had the choice of three classes of comfort of travel on the railway companies' rolling stock.

101. This train stands on the 'up' platform of the Brecon and Merthyr line, a route that was said to be one of the most interesting in South Wales, travelling from Newport through the industrious valleys and onward through the outstanding rural scenery of Breconshire. The last journey on this line was the inspiration of a recorded song that some readers may have heard called *'The Last Train to Torpantau'* all in the spirit of the sound of the train and recording its stops on the way.

102. The romance of steam power is reflected once again on the Penallta branch during the 1950s as a passenger train bound for Dowlais (Cae Harris) pulls into Ystrad Mynach station. Just below the name board can be seen the main station on the Rhymney Valley line.

103. A view looking northwards along the platforms of Hengoed Low Level station with a fully laden coal train making its way down the valley. The board advises that passengers should change here for journeys on the Pontypool and Neath line from the high level and quite often trains would wait for each other's arrival for the convenience of the travelling public.

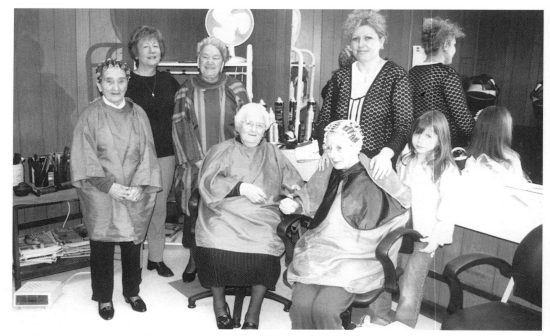

104. Some delighted customers who regularly attend the Headwardian Hair Salon, Hengoed are pictured here with stylists Margaret and Siân. This has been a local hairdressers since 1960 before which it was a small dwelling and linen shop, whilst next door some may remember another small shop owned by Mr. Ali Singh who would be seen roaming the streets selling his wares. In the picture above are Lily Coles, Margaret Williams, Marion Bassett, Miss Lewis, Mrs. James, Siân and a young Cara-Leigh.

105. A long-running and widely popular open-day event is the annual Bedwellty Show, the first one being held at Pontllanfraith in 1873 and then moving to a different location thereafter: Maesycwmmer hosted the event in 1883 and Ystrad Mynach in 1964. Pictured above are members of the Millennium Committee, most of whom are local people and who have enjoyed a long and proud association with the show and they are Arthur Davies, Alwyn Raymond, G. Davies, W. Jenkins, H. Williams (Vice Chairman), O. Watts, J. Jones, R. Ruff, D. Williams, E. Woosnam, B. Penrose, R. Davies, C. Turner, Mrs. E. Jarrold, Mrs. D. James, Mrs. L. Ruff, Alan Biggs, Miss T. Hodge (President), H. Harris (Vice President), S. Turner (Secretary), Colonel M. Jones, S. Barton, M. Lane, C. James.

106. It's a long way from Bardi in Italy to the Beech Tree Fish Bar in Ystrad Mynach and the Platoni family are proud of their pioneering forebears who made that journey. In the 1920s photograph above is Angelo who came to the district in 1906 at the age of 13. Through much hard work the family was very successful in opening fish and chip shops and typical Italian cafés with sons Giuseppe and Guido quickly learning the trade.

107. Over the years the Platoni family moved between Ebbw Vale, Aberbargoed and Blackwood before opening their Ystrad Mynach premises in 1984. Maintained to the high standards set out over the years, this interior view from 2004 shows Giuseppe working alongside son Angelo with assistant Mary.

108. An important event has been recorded in this picture taken at Hayward's Farm in Cefn Hengoed in 1930 - the birth of a calf with Cliff Hayward in attendance and on the right is Elsa Dorkings holding a youngster of the human kind. The farm was later to become the first Lindsay Club and was situated between the Cross Keys and Hengoed Baptist Chapel.

109. Animal lovers may well recognize this photograph of Derek Overton Packer M.R.C.V.S. After leaving Pontypridd Grammar School he entered the Royal Veterinary College London in1943, graduating in 1948 then setting up his practice at Rockland's Ystrad Mynach in 1949. Beginning in a small way, dealing mainly with farm animals, the practice was the first in South Wales to be equipped with an X-ray unit leading to further development for the care of more domestic animals. A founder member of the British Small Animal Veterinary Association, London, Derek became the first President of the South Wales Region and was closely associated with the Ministry of Agriculture as a local inspector of farm animals, particularly during the successful battle against T.B. amongst cattle in the early 1960s. Also recognized as a talented photographer, he is a member of the Royal Photographic Society often presenting slide shows of his work around Europe and beyond.

CHAPTER 5

Matters of Religion

110. The ornate lych gate of Ystrad Mynach's Holy Trinity Church with some parishioners standing by some fifty years ago and although often used as an attractive backdrop for wedding photographs, the lych gate's original purpose is a little more morose. The word lych is an old name for a corpse and the roofed gate was designed to provide shelter for the deceased's coffin during inclement weather whilst waiting for the priest and funeral cortege prior to the service and interment.

111. A picturesque view of Holy Trinity Church, Ystrad Mynach and showing the vicarage at the top left hand corner. The view is typical of how rural the village was until the development of this area during the 1960s. The Trinity fields in the foreground hosted the East Glam show for many years and attracted thousands of people for the event.

112./113. Ystrad Mynach Church has been open for worship since 1857 and like many other such institutions, some 150 years on would not survive without the help of its devotees. Above are members of the Mothers Union, often called the backbone of the church, providing most valuable support within the community. The picture was taken in 1948 and some of the ladies accompanying Vicar Lawrence include Mrs. Lawrence, Mrs. Darcy Waters, Mrs. Evans, Mrs. Petet, Mrs. Emlyn Lloyd, Miss Thomas, Mrs. Cecil, Mrs. Smith of Station Road, Mrs. Hearn and Gladys Herbert.

114. A latter day impressive church building in Maesycwmmer was All Saints which was built in Victoria Road and just to the left of the picture would be the viaduct. All Saints was demolished and a sad loss to the village.

115. Pictured at Moriah Church on Tuesday March 8th 1949 are members of the local Welcome and Hospitality Committee of the Caerphilly National Eisteddfod. With most of the names known they include Rev. Cradoc Owen (guest of honour), Miss Dwynwen Jones, Miss E. Thomas, Mrs. B. Jenkins, Mrs. Lloyd, Miss G. Thomas, Miss Kate Richards, Mrs. I. Williams, Mr. and Mrs. D.W. Davies, Mrs. B. Phillips, Mrs. E. Phillips, Mrs. Yeo, Rev. O. Llew Jeffreys, Mrs. Jeffreys, Mr. D.J. Owen, Mr. T. Erasmus, Mrs. J. Davies, Mrs. H. Williams, Mrs. Humphries, Miss L. Evans, Mrs. J.P. Jones, Miss Dilys Jones and Miss J. Jones. The Welcome Committee includes Mrs. R.H. Williams Hengoed House, (Chairperson), Mrs. L. Fletcher Davies and Miss T.B. Davies (Vice Chairpersons), Miss E. Rowlands (Treasurer), Miss Dwynwen Jones (Secretary), Mrs. Bailey, Mrs. Silas Evans, Dwynwen Morgan, Mrs. Emlyn Lloyd, Mrs. June Evans and Mrs. Jeffries Jones.

116. One church that is still standing in Maesycwmmer is Zoar Presbyterian situated in Commercial Street. This church was built in 1906 as a replacement for the original Zoar that was built much earlier in 1863 at the top end of the village and is noted for its Choral Society, a valuable part of the church's history.

117. Now just another thing of the past as far as local religious feelings are concerned are the annual Whitsun chapel walkabouts. Full of song and brand new clothes to wear, followed by high teas and games, children and adults paraded the streets for all to see and hear. This gathering from Bethany Chapel is pictured during the 1950s at the corner of Lewis Street and Central Street, Ystrad Mynach and a few faces have been recognized to include Susan Hellings, Pamela Amor, Peter Lockyer and Mrs. Hellings.

118. The history of Hengoed Welsh Baptist Chapel reaches back into the 17th century and this photograph was taken in about 1910. The building has received a number of repairs and improvements over the years, the most recent being in 2001 when after extensive work, a service of re-dedication was held in September of that year. Deacons Ann Williams and Mair Probert are proud of the work carried out with the help of public funding and friends of the building who call themselves 'Hen Dy Cwrdd' which translated means 'Old Meeting Place'.

119. Momentous celebrations were held at the chapel in 1950 as demonstrated by the crowd seen here and amongst the many who attended were Mr. and Mrs. Johnny Walters, Mr. and Mrs. Tommy Walters, Mr. and Mrs. Emrys Phillips and Mr. Brynmor Davies.

120./121. Harvest Festival time is another important date in the chapel calendar as will be seen in this interior view of Tabor which was rebuilt into its present form in 1876. These two pictures were taken in 1925 and many of the names below have been recalled for the occasion such as Joe Hamilton, Ada Thomas, John Thomas, Nathan Osborne, Jack Davies, May Roberts, Doris Roberts, Edith Roberts, Gwyneth Osborne, Margery Harris, Marjorie Clark, Betty Osborne, Cassie Herbert, Rene Rees, Brenda Williams, Norah Mills, Ethel Phillips, Tommy Williams, Malcolm Williams, Howell Thomas, Kenny Maddock, Ivor Phillips, Harry Rees and Geoff Clark.

122./123. Bethania Chapel in Twyn Road Ystrad Mynach during the 1950s and the Sunday School pupils seen below have just completed their annual Whitsun Walk. After the Whitsun Walk there was a tea party and games which were held in the 'Tumpy' field, now the site of the college. They include Basil Jenkins, Janet McCarthy, Lorraine Atwood, Howard Summers, Joyce Morgan, Jill Manning, Jane Jenkins, Nigel Jarman, ? Jenkins, Ivor Jenkins, Ronald Jones, Gerald Jones. Siân McCarthy, Heather Murphy, Betty Jenkins, Cathy Atwood, Kathleen Jones, Pauline Jenkins, Anita Sparey, Ann Harris, Pat Tudor. Mimi Skrbic, Christine Summers, Julia Osolinski, June Osolinski, Paul Lewis and Susan Meads.

124. Hengoed Tabernacle English Baptist Church began life on October 21st 1905 with a membership of 30 worshippers at the rear of Brooklands, the home of Mr. and Mrs. A.L. Morgan of Maesycwmmer and is seen in this photograph. In early 1906 work had commenced on a more permanent chapel to house a growing congregation and this was officially opened in October of that year.

125. The newly completed Tabernacle. Its first minister was a Mr. Arthur Harris and church records from the period mention that a leading lady was a Mrs. A.L. Morgan, who formed a Christian Endeavour Society much to the appreciation of the young people of the area now that they had a permanent place of worship. Unfortunately in 2001 structural damage to the building was discovered and thus the chapel was forced to close its doors. A special service of praise and thanksgiving was held on June 30th 2001 led by Rev. J. Randal Morgan assisted by Peter Manson and Rev. Geoffrey J. Tyson.

CHAPTER 6

Schooldays

126. Although almost eighty years old, this school photograph from Ystrad Mynach has revealed some of the pupils' names who may well have descendants now in possession of this book and those known are Roy Robins, Trevor Robins, Alec Harris, ? Pullen, Hugh Edwards, Ivor Thomas (Ystrad Fawr), Arthur Mallon, Reggie Davies, Mr. (Jackie) Morgan - Deputy Head, Cyril Bernard, Jack Hopkins, Dick Rowlands, Bobby Dyke and Melvin Davies.

127. Pupils of the same school are now pictured during the 1950s and as only a few names have been traced, readers will need to do a little homework themselves to try and identify a few faces! Those that are known include Billy Jones, John Drayton, Clive Howells, Charlie George, Tommy Holmes, William Skyrme, Kenny Cross, David Edwards, Ceirog Jones, Mrs. Edwards, Pat Holloway, Pat Richards, Olga Warne, Betty Reeks, Georgina Weeks, Pat Price, Rita Everson, Pam Jones and Edwina Edwards.

128. Ystrad Mynach Junior School in the late 1950s and on this occasion most of the pupils' names are known (left to right). Back: Adrian Anderson, Alan Jones, David Kozlowski, Susan Martin, Jennifer Davies, Maureen Waite, Helen Jones, Ashley Williams, Hugh Evans. Middle: Howard Evans, Howard Williams, Billy Beer, Peter Lockyer, Keith Williams, David James, Richard Teconi, John Jones, Karl Evans. Front: Elaine Weaver, Jean Phillips, Marilyn Jones, Maria Evans, Jeanette Scott, Dorothy ?, Mary Owen, Carol Dinecombe, Marilyn Davies, Christine Bosley and Jennifer Beacham.

129. More 1950s pupils at the school are to be found here with apologies to those whose names have been omitted. Back: unknown, Calvin Williams, Gwyn Williams, Richard Scott, Ian Clark, Duncan Smith, Michael Clifford. Middle: John Mathews, Peter Ash, Malcolm Williams, Susan Bitel, Kay Phillips, Pamela Hadden, Susan Case, Jeffrey Kent, John Morgan, Charles Davies. Front: Lynne Thomas, Pamela Jones, Marilyn Harding, Janice Hayter, Christene Summers, Linda Gatrill, Lyn Edwards, Helena Drobisz, Caroline Hughes, Ann Richards and Margaret Murray.

130. One more from the 1950s period at Ystrad Mynach and hopefully there are some readers that will recognize an old school friend or two. Back: Tony Andrews, Philip Biggs, Terry Winwood, unknown, Philip Evans, Terry Proudly, Glen Vaughan, Peter Lessimore, Clive Williams, Mrs. Phillips. Middle: Alan Thomas, Tony James, Judith Evans, Kay Nash, Lorraine Hoskins, Bridget Evans, Janet Sheen, Janet James, Elizabeth Mallon, Michael James, Andrew Parry. Front (Girls): Elizabeth Richards, Janet Weaver, Lorna Evans, Gaynor Hook, Pamela Davies, Judith Lewis, Lorraine Williams, Lynette Morris, Joyce Evans, Carol Burke. Boys: Lawrence Anderson, Michael Doran and David Lucas.

131. The period has now moved on to the 1970s and in the picture are - Back: Christine Morgan, Lenny Oliver, Geraint Edwards, Nadia Murphy, Tina Lucklow, Kevin Morgan, Susan Chamberlain, Michael Williams, Stephen Morgan, Carol Cushion, Mr. Paul Blewitt. Middle: Jeffrey Stonehedge, Julie Price, Huw Jones, Andrew Paget, Stephen Murphy, Julie Moss, Norma Walker, Andrew Williams, David Jones, Philip Hearne, Marvin Saunders. Front: Lyn Shemwell, Frances ?, Nadia Chin, Mary Davies, Lesley Davies, David Davies, Andrew Davies, Lyndon Ennis, Michael Guilfoyle and Michael Davies.

132. Even more up to date as we see the Junior School, Standard 4 Year 6 1988-89 and for the camera are - Back: Mr. Gwenlan (Head Teacher), Ross Jenner, Stephen Ramsay, Alan George, Allem Din, Steven Lewis, Clint Williams, Dale Tucker, Mr. Rees (Deputy Head Teacher). Middle: Martin Rowe, Mark James, David Edwards, Sarah Lloyd, Rachel Griffiths, Laura Joshi, Emma West, Helen Clark, Yvonne West, Ian Young, Martin Cushion. Front: Bethan Jenkins, Rosemary Gwynn, Elizabeth Grey, Natalie Jones, Sarah Harvey, Katherine Hopkinson, Nia Williams, Helen Edwards, Emma Tudor and Emma Carey.

133. Back to the fifties just once more for this collection of Ystrad Mynach Junior pupils as follows - Back: Mansel Williams, David Morgan, Roger Nelmes, Raymond Silverthorne, Richard Adams, Malcolm Deeks, Stephen Dunn, Michael Samuel, Andrew Mullins, Howard Evans, Roger Griffiths, Kenneth Harding, Peter Bowden. Middle: unknown, Robert Layton, Kay Poulson, unknown, unknown, Jennifer Nash, Janet Gerrish, Angela Snook, unknown, Marilyn Ashcroft, Jean Loader, Dilys Osborne, Alison Williams, Adrian Beacham, Graham Payne. Front: Janet Price, Pauline Jenkins, Catherine Thomas, Susan Jones, Eileen Jones, Linda Pavey, Susan Williams, Wendy Haggett, Yvonne Wyatt, Shirley Rowlands, Mr. Evans and Haydn Smith.

134. Hengoed School 1926 with teachers Miss Edmunds and Miss Herwin. Many of the children's names are given and include Olive Anderson, Dorothy Meads, Maud Norman, Eunice Campbell, Lavinia Gardener, Betty Evans, Joan Bailey, Marion Meads, Master George, Phyllis Keen, Nancy Beard, Nesta Jones, Gladys Herbert, Betty Evans, Evelyn Powell, Sarah Tossell, Master George, Betty White, Dilys Evans, Margaret Baker, Gertie Wilson, Nancy Kent, Dylis Tuck, Jimmy Edwards, Ron Whittle, ? Andrews, Hector Jones, Ken Jones, Harold Brooks, Tommy Edwards, Cyril Jones, Leonard Syers, Hugh Jones, Leonard Gower and R. Syers.

135. The boys at Hengoed School twenty years later in 1946 with - Back: D.J. Owen, ? Sullivan, Ron Powell, G. James, Terry Powell, Gren Jones, Mr. Webb. 2nd Row: ? Paget, John Carney, Teddy Jenkins, Ken Griffiths. 3rd and 4th Rows: Len Capel, Roy Evans, Grenville Davies, Colin Skinner, Freddy Cross, unknown, Brian Nash, Alan Thomas, Gerald Harris, Colin Williams, Des Clark, Les Dunn, David Lane and Danny Ireland.

136. Hengoed Junior School in 1955 with teacher Mr. Hayes and headmaster Mr. Owen. Left to right, the pupils are Row 4 (Back): Neil Rhys, John Macullam, Jeffrey Williams, Roger Woods, Marlene Jones, Moira Garbett, Trevor Davies, John Godsall, Kenny Jenkins, Raymond Dare. Row 3: Gwyneth Morgan, Gwyneth Holland, Margaret Ellis, Pamela Powell, Valerie Wilson, Heather Kinsley, Diane Monkton, Margaret Briggs, Diane Jenkins, Helen Price. Row 2: Rosemary Gerrett, Wendy Arthur, Phyllis Morgan, Ann Harris, Diane Hegarty, Janice Preston, Ann Grayson, Christine ?, Jean Griffiths, Janet Gamble, Jennifer Jones. Front: Douglas George, Lyn Gittins, David Male, Gwyn Jones, Michael Taylor and Roger Pyke.

137. Again the mid 1950s with teacher Miss Williams and head Mr. Owen in charge. The pupils are Back: Dennis Livingstone, Roy Barry, Lyndon Williams, Graham Grayson, Howard Lane, Kenny James, Geoffrey Holder, Alan Mills, Eugene Marriott, Andrew Costa. Middle: Michael Dolloway, Ken Pascoe, Emlyn Webb, Trevor Courts, Melvin Davies, David Packham, Malcolm Langley, Hayden Ruck, Jeffrey Rodway, David Powell. Front: Jennifer James, Irene Padfield, Janette Holmes, Sylvia Stephens, Betty Piper, Brenda Gittens, June Baxendale, Anita Meyrick, Angela Roles, Margaret Lewis and Betty Bishop.

138. Now in the late fifties and teacher Mrs. Pearce is photographed with her pupils. Back: unknown, Tony Costa, Neil Boardman, Steve Jenkins, Kevin Hughes, Steve Goodenough, Colin ?, Malcolm ?, Gareth Preece. Middle: Marie King, Ken Briggs, unknown, David Taylor, Jean Northam, Joy Cooper, Robert Old, Phillip Mills, Mostyn Williams. Front: Ann Pardoe, Siân Gittens, Ann Rogers, Susan Amor, Carol Powell, Denise Mills, Ann Davies, Lynette Skidmore, Vicky Ellis, Valerie Jones, Elizabeth Williams and Betty Boobier.

139. The year is now 1960 at Hengoed School with the following names to look out for - Back: Mr. Owen, Stuart Baker, David Ellis, Jeffrey Woods, Peter Christopher, Eric Pardoe. Middle: Alan James, Brian Adams, Ronald George, Jean Macdonald, Heather Price, Meryl Evans, Martin Jones, Malcolm Burgin, Martin Pask, Mrs. Pearce. Front: Tina Lachno, Julie Bellamy, Sandra Thomas, Avril Price, Jacqueline Eddington, Gwyneth Parry, Susan Lacey, Sheila Whitefoot, Susan Hughes, Pat Jenkins and Irene Briggs.

140. A Derwendeg School photograph that includes - Back: Ceridwen Vivian, Nita James, Muriel Jones, Gill Edwards, Dennis Price, Pearl George, Dennis Cushion, David Williams. Middle: Jean Price, Maureen Carney, Olive Bolter, unknown, Eric Evans, Gwyn James, Cled Williams, Clive Jones, Betty Jay, Kathleen Cullen. Front: Colin Dolloway, unknown, Elton Hart, Raymond Jones, Verdun Bowden, Jenny Elliott, Brenda Furber, ? McCarthy, Haydn Herbert, Gwyneth Price, Frank Israel and Mavis Paget.

141. Derwendeg in 1958. Back: Steven Ross, Adrian Philpott, Robert Mazurczak, Royston Oliver, Raymond Brown, Richard Whittle, John Williams, Bernard Meredith, unknown, Michael Gilbert, Mike O'Connell. Middle: Philip Smith, Alan Davies, Steven Edmunds, Janice Woodyatt, Eileen Cullen, Marion Haines, Paul Green, Billy Davies (Piano), Terry Yorath, Terry Jones, Alan Jones. Front: Lorraine Baines, Maureen Price, Linda Saunders, Carol Tucker, Susan Davies, Katrina Rupnik, Susan Taylor, Marion Hurley, Odette White, Susan Phillips, Carol Summers, Maureen Vivian, Cynthia Griffiths. In the very front are Michael Mackenzie, Barry Lewis and Michael Tipper.

142. A 1957 picture from the same school with the following - Back: Michael Caple, Paul Wangiel, Paul Jaskola, Alan Price, George Purnell, unknown, Elaine Buckley, Ivor Young, Ronnie Willetts, Ray Tapper. Middle: Paul McCarthy, John Dexter, ? Roberts, Jackie Hughes, Henry Smiga, Joyce Evans, Ellien Meara, Janet Garda, unknown, Vanessa Jones, Susan Powell, Ann Woods. Front: unknown, Doug Mackenzie, Haydn Warburton, Desmond Clark, Keith Pope, Leslie Wallbank, Sandra Roberts, Barbara Woods, Sherry Jones, unknown, unknown and Eileen James.

143. Headmaster Mr. Evans and teacher Mrs. Williams accompany this Derwendeg School photograph from the late 1950s. Back: Michael Reeks, Clive Thomas, Robert Wood, Ron Corbin, Raymond James, Gary Biggs, Kenneth Pritchard, Alan Sharp, Terry Warburton, Dai Lewis. Middle: Ken Pope, Lyndon Matthews, Gwilym Jones, Steven Crocker, Peter Winters, Dennis Smith, Ken Walker, Robert Long, Ken Fowler, Tommy Reeks. Front: Margaret Lewis, Brenda Atkinson, Rosmond Jones, Diane Weyman, Susan Morris, Jean Dunn, Christine Phillips, Lyn Holmes, Rowena Griffiths, Carol Hinwood and Susan Matthews.

144. Moving on to the 1970s and the children at Derwendeg are dressed for an old time musical performance and to be picked out in the crowd are Joanne Jenkins, Sarah George, Zoe James, Karen Crumb, Adele Osbourne, Ruth Marriott, Paul Cheverton, Claire Arnott, Tara Griffiths, Lisa Morgan, Martine Morris, Marie Colyer, Andrew Catlin, Shaun O'Connor, Marie Stacey, Claire Feeley, Ellen Showell, Leka Walker, Toni Jones, Pauline Meredith, Lee Williams, Lisa Wood, Colleen Osbourne, Maria Jones and Helen Arnold.

145. Showtime again at the same school and this time it's the 1980s for a performance of The Wizard of Oz. Back: unknown, Alan Tinkler, unknown, Darren Weyman, Gareth Hall, unknown. Middle: Joanne Jenkins, Jamie Duggan, Lee Williams, Debbie Wilding, Sarah George, Maria Jones, Marie Colyer, unknown, unknown, Leka Walker. Front: unknown, Richard Lewis, Nobby Long and Kelly Walters.

146. This scene was taken outside the entrance to Maesycwmmer School in 1931 but unfortunately only a few names have come to light and they are Mr. Alf Probert (teacher), Tommy Jordan, Georgie Brice, Malcolm Williams (the farm), Ethel Phillips and Doreen Cox.

147. In the Maesycwmmer School yard and the pupils are - Back: Steven Lewis, Brian Powell, Wayne Moses, Les Hewer, Stephen Bryant, Steven Harry, Jonathan Rao, Colin Snook, Simon Ward, Mrs. Boyle. Row 3: Jayne Fedstone, Michelle Meredith, Pat Ilsley, Ceri ?, Gillian Haynes, Lynne Wilson, Caroline Oram, Caroline Blake, unknown. Row 2: Tina Elliott, Gaynor Boulton, Elaine Thomas, Helen Buckland, Sandra Whittaker, Julie Meyrick, June Hewer, Lynne Sullivan, Maria Shymanski. Front: Anthony Elliott, Byron Roberts, Martin Thomas, Kevin Tinklin, Mark Harries, Elwyn Williams and Wayne Edmunds.

148. From about 1970 is this Maesycwmmer picture with - Back: Mark Burnell, Andrew Jenkins, Darren White, Douglas Davies, Jeremy Plange, Malcolm Davies, Andrew Owen, Ian Tedstone. Row 3: Christopher Davies, Jason Love, Mark Fisher, Janet Clark, Mandy O'Brien, Caroline Powell, Alison Jones, Angela Jones, Nigel Davies, Andrew Edwards, Andrew Illsley and teacher Mrs. J. Davies. Row 2: Sharon Davies, Karen Davies, Janet Mote, Lynne Williams, Helen Taylor, Gaynor Fennell, Joanne Dawney, Margaret Baker, Susan Davies. Front: Derek Meyrick, Andrew Brimble, John Fever, Lyndon Davies and Miles Bailey.

149. Again from the 1970s at the school are - Back: unknown, Gareth Williams, Colin Elliott, Christopher Thomas, Stephen King, Mark Davies, Trevor Fennell, unknown, John Williams and Mr. Jenkins. Row 3: Christopher Powell, Derek Oram, Christine Ward, Christine Powell, Gaynor Saunders, Avril Elliott, Trudy Oram, Michael Gammon, Alan Williams. Row 2: Sheila Whittaker, Josie Rao, Ceri Speirs, Anita Phillips, unknown, Maureen Elliott, Denise Roper, Susan Mote, Theresa Roper. Front: John Tudball, Michael Boulton, Steven Anderson, Derek Walters, Ian Jones, unknown.

150. St. David's Day is as always Welsh costume day in the schools and these two pictures are from Maesycwmmer Junior in the 1970s and in amongst the crowd are Sarah James, Lisa Nottingham, Donna Cory, Andrea James, Helen Gibbon, ? Evans, Ceri Sellick, Amanda Tanner, Amanda ?, Maria Rees, Sharon Chaplin, Lynette Davies, Phillipa Walker, Lynne Casley, Catherine Cook, Lisa Tudor, Louise Garrett, Georgina Nash, Tracey Tudor and Ceri Hussain.

151. Some more traditional Welsh fashion is seen here with Ruth Gibbon, Nicola Davies, Phillipa Walker, Sharon Chaplin, Catherine Cook, Lynette Davies, Deborah Meyrick, David Lawrence, Richard Barnham, Lisa Faloon, Ian Morgan, Stephen Francis and Mark Holly.

152. The Junior School once more in celebratory dress with their teacher. Back: Huw Evans, Gareth Whittaker, Stephen Jones, Andrew Fisher, John Downer, Mathew Tucker, Thomas ?, Dean Davies, Michael Hayes, Martin Male. Middle: Claire Tudball, Michelle Brideaux, Kathryn Miller, Rashma Patel, Andrea Woodyatt, Sharon Brideaux, Donna Bishop, Justine Griffin. Front: Robert Moffat, Lee Sellick, Derrick Snook, Mark Jex, Linda Illsley, Helen Dyer, Sean Nicholas, Roland Humphries.

153. The final photograph in this chapter comes from Maesycwmmer School in the 1950s and where known, the pupils' names are given. Back: Keith ?, Gerald Pugh, Dennis Leonard, unknown, Ian Brimble, Reg Salmon, Colin James, unknown, unknown, unknown. Row 3: Barry Clulow, Carol Pritchard, Sandra Cook, Viska Wallach, Pamela Williams, Jacqueline Gibbs, Mavis McPherson, Christine Bradfield, Gwyneth Hatton, David Jones. Row 2: Susan Williams, Janice Lewis, Diane ?, Freda Weeks, unknown, unknown, Jennifer ?, Maxine Davies, Mary Barnett, Ann Brideaux, Christine Richards. Sitting: unknown, William Eastman and unknown.

CHAPTER 7

Sport and Recreation

154. Some highly professional club members who were former players took it upon themselves to create a 'Sporty' calendar for Penallta Rugby Club for the year 2003 as seen in these two excerpts. The expertise of Mike Guilfoyle of 'Splash Design', Dino Spinetti of 'Hanbury Photography' and club photographer and Martin Roe created a hugely popular memento. For November Steven Cribb is delighted to have the Penallta-Etts to ensure that he is washed in all the right places assisted by Nicola Brown, Nicola Sullivan, Louise Morgan, Joanne Rowe, Nicole Owen, Louise Rees and Nicola Cottier.

155. For December Mike Guilfoyle has just scored a try with Mark Griffiths looking on and is only too willing to allow Welsh Rugby legend Neil Jenkins to take the conversion. The game was Newbridge RFC versus Penallta Select XV with a number of guest players all in aid of the 'Robert Moore Appeal Fund'.

156. A Graddfa School, Ystrad Mynach rugby photograph that goes back to the 1960s with the following boys and staff member. Back: Brian Prosser, Neil Grey, John Morgan, Keith Parker, Richard Herold, Dai Kozlowski, Alan Hayter, Alan Griffiths, Billy Holton, Beverly Davies, Brent Perrott, Dai Evans, Alan Evans, Mr. Rees, Glen Rogers, Alan Thomas, Howard Williams, David James (Jako), John Matthews (Oxo), Gareth Silcox and Neil Coles.

157. Ystrad Mynach 'Old Boys' formed what was to be regarded as the best team in the Rhymney Valley, winning many trophies such as the treble seen here and an achievement rarely matched. The picture is from poorer times when only the black shorts were provided, the players having to supply their own white shirts! Reading from the back are Leonard Perriman, Bernard Martin (Sec), Granville Davies, Terry Frowen, Terry Caple, John Williams, Doug Powell, Brian Darcy, Bob Perriman, Bill Moore, Mr.Caple, John Perriman, ? Phillips, unknown, Vernon Jenkins, Clive Edwards, Ray Bishop and Dave Beynon.

158. On the left is a former and one of the best 'Maesycwmmer Mountain Fighters' alias boxer Doug Walker of Gellihaf. Between 1937 and 1939 Doug fought 43 matches, losing only 2 and by almost everyone, these were regarded as very poor decisions, he holding the distinction of never having been knocked to the canvas during this period. Boxing in booths at £5 a time, he was constantly approached by someone who wanted to have a go, and was known to always carry a tin of Vaseline in his pocket for eye protection in case of an unexpected fight. Would-be boxers hoping to make a name for themselves, would travel for miles knocking on his door proposing a challenge to this much-feared local champion who also had the reputation of being the number one tram-filler on his shift when working at Penallta Colliery.

159. Cefn Hengoed Lindsay Scotland Trip 1987. Back row: Andrew O'Halloran, Russell Cuddihy, Dean George, Nigel Stacey, Steve Davies, John Southall, Phillip Jones, Mark Ives. 2nd Row: Billy Vivian, Ken Cross, John Wilding, Vic Clark, Mickey Lewis, Adrian Anderson, Dai Clark, Steve Pennell. Seated: Glyn Wilding, Lee Cushing, Albert Wilding, Viv Clapham, Doug George, Gary Humphries, Trevor Davies, Arthur Amos. In front: John Jay, Alan Day and Rocky George.

160./161. Ystrad Mynach Bowls Club had celebrated its 75th anniversary in 2002 having established themselves as a well-respected and highly-motivated club, with many successes to their credit. Two of the club's singles champions for 2003 are seen here - Idris Penrose and Kath Poulton, the anniversary champions to be mentioned were Gareth Davies and Pamela Penrose.

162. This is the anniversary photograph from 2002 and from the top left are L. Davies, H. Evans, D. Lewis, C. Sellick, K. Godsall, B. Reynolds, A. Reynolds, C. Thomas, T. Maslen, Ian Thomas, D. Parry, R. Thomas, J. Knight, T. Andrews, L. Wells, C. Andrews, D. Taylor, D. Bennett, T. Richards, L. Sexon, T. Sullivan, G. Phillips, J. Perkins, P. McDougall, T. Nutt, G. Vaughan, G. Alderman, A. Berry, W.R. Williams, T. Bouse, J. Perrott, T. Bird, G.M. Jones (Treas.), V. Morgan (life mem.), I. Penrose (Vice Chair), B. Greenaway (Capt.), J. Davies (Chair), A. Donaldson (Council Chair), K. Cooper (Pres.), T. Everson (Fix Sec), D. Morgan (Sec), L. John (2nd Team Capt), G.T. Davies (Anniv. Chair), D. Davies, R. Parry, J. Cross, G. Davies, R. Rudge, P. Elsworth, R.A. Cook, T.J. Davies, T. Matthews, G. Williams, L. Cory, C. Williams and C. Edwards.

163./164. These two photographs from the 1920s and 1930s illustrate the archway of roses and flower beds that were once the pride and joy of the groundsman at Ystrad Mynach Welfare Ground. The archway led to the bowling green, whilst the sports pavilion, a prominent feature of the park was destroyed by fire in the 1960s.

165. The Don and Cribbage champions of the Butchers Arms in Maesycwmmer are seen here in the late 1970s displaying their championship cup and trophies. They are B. Price, B. Rogerstone, G. Morgan, B. Powell, J. Church, C. Taylor, P. James, B. Garrett, T. Casley, P. McDougall, J. Evans, K. Milton, M. Roberts, E. Hughes, T. Roberts, A. Seer, C. Moon, A. James, M. Knott and M. Price.

166. The Ystrad Mynach Old Boys Committee are pictured here with their display of cups won during the 1970s and they include Tanner Davies, Allan Rogers, Keith Roberts, M. Pritchard, Trevor Everson, Lenny Fowler, Brian Hart, Peter Hegarty, Alan Livingstone, David Beynon, unknown.

167. Adrian and David Barwood of Maesycwmmer were two outstanding sportsmen, representing Wales in athletics and rugby and they are seen here being actively involved with the coaching and playing of the village rugby team in the 1980s. In the frame left to right are Back: Finlay Beaton, unknown, Anthony Lewis, Bret Jenkins, Peter ?, Paul Ferris, Andrew Coles, Gary Jones, John Evans, John Davies, Alan ?, Geraint Roberts, Dean Davies, Ken Sullivan. Front: Adrian Barwood, Ian Furmage, Andrew Fletcher, Keith Perkins, David Barwood, Phil Long, Steve Chidgey, Stephen Jones, Gareth ? and Daniel Barwood.

168. A football match between Hengoed Old Boys and Bargoed is seen at Hengoed football field during the 1960s, with a rare view of the Institute that was used for numerous functions including boxing tournaments. Some may also remember the old tin shed at the bottom of the Welfare Ground used as the players' changing room and the accompanying tin baths. Here, back in March 1955, a future international snooker champion by the name of Ray Reardon was making a name for himself in the finals of the Rhymney Valley League, playing J. Cusack of Deri. Players on the field in this photograph include Ray Bishop (left), Ralph Davies and Dai Beynon.

169. Ystrad Mynach Boys and Girls Club which was formed in Lewis Street, celebrates its 70th year in this group photograph. The present club leader Ken Pritchard is pictured with officials Tony Honeywill, Dave Hurley, Tom Pritchard and numerous helpers. Ken and wife Sylvia having worked hard for the club have since received good news regarding funding that will secure much refurbishment; the following few photographs illustrate the interest taken by members of the club.

170. Presentation night at the Boys Club in the early 1970s with Mal Court, Curly Morgan, Gareth Hopkins, Paul Craven, Gary Caple, John Gateaux, Paul Thomas, Mike Elliott, Philip Yorath, Nigel Beynon, Derrick Hughes, Colin Williams, Clive Mathews, Howard Beynon and Andrew Mulvey.

171. The Boys Club Under 16s League winners 1961/62 are seen here having contributing another win to the club's history. Seen are P. Thomas (Leader), G. Jonathon, Brian Harris, Len Fowler, Alan Williams, Graham Harris, Gary Williams, Alfie Brownsword, Mike Rice, Joe Brownsword, Trevor Williams, Idris Penrose, Dennis Jones, Roger Williams and Brian Rich.

172. Another successful team from the memorable years of the 1960s with - Back: David Thomas, Jeff Rees, Keith Williams, Robert Lancaster, Phillip Amos, Gareth Silcox, Brian Hart. Middle: Ronnie Mee, Alan Jones, Len Hussey, Paul Jones, Peter Thomas, Brian Prosser, Billy Beer. Front: John Hughes, Maldwyn Thomas, Howard Jones (Chippy).

173. Ystrad Mynach Junior School, Lewis Street has been the starting point for many talented individuals in sport and on-going careers. The photograph here is of a junior netball B team in the 1987/88 season and the girls are - Back: Ruth Morgan, Emma West, Juliet Larson, Emma Tudor, Andrea Lewis. Front: Nia Williams, Dawn Davies and Leanne Cole.

174. The senior hockey team of Ystrad Mynach Lewis Girls' Comprehensive School in 2000 when they were National Urdd Champions and third in the National Schools Championship. The team consists of Carmen Hayes, Adrianne Maslen, Hannah Mead, Kate Davies, Katrin Budd, Claire Gannon, Kathryn Elliott, Joanne Rowe, Laura Hempstead, Claire Mackenzie, Sarah Rawlings, Sarah Vaughan and Cerys Jenkins.

CHAPTER 8

Personalities and Events

175. Colonel Henry Edzell Morgan Lindsay of Ystrad Fawr, an acclaimed soldier, politician and sportsman. He was the son of Lieutenant Colonel H.C. Lindsay of Glasevin House, County Dublin, the family being part members of a great Scottish clan of the same name and the Lindsays were very much part of everyday life in the Ystrad Mynach area. The colonel was a noted trainer, steeplechase rider and breeder of Kerry hill sheep but above all, particularly respected as a family for their generosity and care towards the local population. The colonel was destined for a distinguished military career from the start, being educated at the Royal Academy Gosport in Hampshire, from there to the Royal Academy Woolwich and on to the Royal Engineers. Service was spent in the first and last South African Wars and the nineteenth century conflicts in the Sudan. These experiences helped him towards a Knight of the Order of St. John, Deputy Lieutenant of Glamorgan, a member of the governing body of the Church in Wales and warden at Holy Trinity Ystrad Mynach. He was to marry Eleen Katherine Thomas, daughter of Mr. G.W.D. Thomas and granddaughter of Reverend Thomas of Llanbradach and Ystrad Fawr, the family having connections with the district for more than six centuries. Colonel Lindsay's mother was also of some distinction, she being the Hon Ellen Sarah Morgan, daughter of the first Lord of Tredegar. Offspring of the couple followed in the footsteps of military service that was to end in great tragedy. During the First World War (1914-1918) the Colonel and his wife suffered incalculably with the loss of three of their sons in battle (a situation that would have been avoided at all cost by today's military leaders); they were Captain George Walter Lindsay, Major Claude Frederick Lindsay and Lieutenant Archibald Lindsay.

176. The perfect platform for a prospective career in the R.A.F. might well be training in the Air Training Corps with members seen here outside the headquarters at the back of Central Street. One of the founders at Ystrad Mynach was Brian Heffron who started as a cadet in 1960 and went through the ranks to become a Warrant Officer; he was a flying cadet from 1962 to 1974 and went further on to become a flying instructor with the South Wales Gliding Club. Some names to look for here include Michael Burgin, David Edmunds, Dennis Summers, Lyn Baker, Michael Mylan, WO Baker, ? Webb, David Morgan, Alan Rudge, Kevin Dorran, Brian Heffron, Malcolm Hester and Flying Officer Burgin.

177. Hayward's Field is the setting for Cefn Hengoed's Carnival Queen in the early 1930s when Irene Lewis won the title. She is accompanied by Phyllis Casley (Flower Girl), Terry Jones (Page Boy) and bridesmaids Maud Williams, Lilly May Phillips, Betty Evans and Renee Price.

178. A firm favourite with many to liven up an event is a local jazz band and this is the Maesycwmmer troupe, Forester Islanders on a carnival day in the 1980s. The players are Sharon Whittaker, Annette Bevan, Sarah Brideaux, Lynette Davies, Sara Wilson, Tracey Tudor, Andrea James, Sarah Hewer, Kristen Baker, David Brideaux, Idris Thomas and Ruth Bennett.

179. During the 1950s and '60s, the Ystrad Mynach Trinity Players Drama Group entertained thousands with their first-class performances of some best-loved plays such as Murder In The Cathedral, See How They Run and Proof Of The Poison to name but a few. Some of the players here are David Morgan, Hilda Watts, Morlais Evans, Peggy Gardner, Audrey Field, Michael Morgan, Allan Forrester, John Gardner, Malcolm Pugh, Ruth Webb, Deidre Perrott, Megan Davies, Joan Steel and Iris Jones.

180. Maesycwmmer Brownies are pictured at one of their summer picnics during the 1950s. The photograph was taken on the old track and was a favourite with the locals as a popular site for camping out. Amongst the girls are Margaret Morris, June Williams, Joan Biggs, Gaynor Morgan, Janet Graham, Margaret Morris (2), Gillian Jones, Lyn Bell, Dilys Harris, Jean Jones, Pat Williams, Mary Davies, Marilyn Chaplin, Jean Morgan, Dorothy John and Cynthia Clark.

181. An inaugural concert was held in November 2002 to mark the opening of the new Lewis School, Pengam with compositions from past and present pupils and staff. Two of the composers Mervyn Burtch and Michael Davies (Young Musician of the Year 2003) are seen with conductor Jane Bell at Ystrad Mynach Library having presented their work for posterity to the library and Tredomen Heritage Museum.

182. The Queen's Golden Jubilee in 2002 is being celebrated by Central Street and Church Street by many including Tracy Bradmore-Lammas, Sue Williams, Jackie Swales, Angela Whittock, Rhys Williams, Daniel Evans, Jane Hayter, Steve Jackson, Joyce Williams, Susan Evans and Simon Evans.

183. The opening of a branch of The Red Cross Society on the site of an old toilet block in Lisburn Road in March 1993 is recognized as a great asset to the community. Founded locally by Mrs. Heulwen Mason and Mrs. Dr. Jones, it is well known for its exceptional abilities in topping the County in fundraising. In the picture are June Hawkins, Yvonne Clarke, Karen Morgan, Pat Jones, Arthur Pugh, Margaret White, Anne James, Mary James, Pat Fluck, Rose Lynne, Marie Wadley, Phyllis Thomas, Elizabeth Strong, Heather Keane, David Holland, Joyce Evans, Beatrice Morgan, Ann Morgan and Dilys Sutton.

184. Another of Ystrad Mynach's long-respected characters was Mr. Evan Richards, pictured alongside his wife Llewela at a function during the 1950s. He will be remembered as the local undertaker and builder for more than 60 years following in his father's footsteps in 1933. As a businessman he played an active part in the local Chamber of Trade, Deacon of Moriah Chapel and during the war years served as a Special Constable in the district. Gifted with an excellent bass voice, he was a member of the Nelson and District Choral Society and president of Bargoed Rotary Club, a position he retained until his death at the grand old age of ninety in 2002.

185. Graddfa School Band, who in the 1960s achieved runner-up position at their very first attempt in the youth section of the National Schools Competition held in London. Many band-members went on to form the Ystrad Mynach District Brass Band and worthy of a mention is the first girl member, Catherine Morgan who was aged just seven! In this picture are Back: David Walters, Malcolm Boucher, Michael Lane, Malcolm Deeks, John Bosley, Kevin Doran. Middle: Graham Barrar (Music Teacher), Lyndon Hughes, Gareth Pugh, Gwyn Fieldhouse, David Morgan, Terry Jones, Alan Langford, Ieuan Morgan (Teacher). Front: Michael Power, Michael Burgin, Philip Andrews, Mr. Williams (Head Teacher), Raymond Silverthorne, Alan Bridges and Michael Yorath.

186. Maesycwmmer Jazz Band during the 1960s. Back: Debbie McDougall, Kerin Maidment, Trudy Oram, Dawn Dawton, June Smith, June Davies, Mara Barbero, Carol Eales, Angela Davies, Trudy Barbero, Caroline Lloyd. Middle: Martine Burnell, Lynne Barbero, Helen Church, Tony Prosser, Gareth Davies, Lyn Peplar, Avril Elliot, Christine Powell, Catherine Hawker. Front: Diane Oram.

187. The year 1935 celebrated the Silver Jubilee of King George V, grandfather to our present Queen and across the country, the lighting of a series of beacons on high points marked the occasion. Ystrad Mynach at the time claimed to have one of the largest and best-constructed for miles around as seen by the work being put into it in this photograph. It was situated at the highest point approx. 1100 ft up on the Eglwyilan mountain above Graddfa Farm and was constructed by the local Toc H scouts with the help of local Tradesmen, Colliery Proprietors, Lorry owners and many others. In the photograph Scoutmaster Henry Frowen can be seen safely at the bottom and Captain Evans at the top of the pile. Over forty tons of combustible material and no less than two hundred gallons of oil were used. The BBC radio signal was relayed by arrangement with Messrs. Morgan and Abbis of Radio House Ystrad Mynach at 10 p.m. when Mr. Douglas A. Hann, M.E. set the giant bonfire alight.

188. More Royal Celebrations took place in 1969 with the Investiture of The Prince of Wales and as part of the local entertainment these Hengoed ladies formed their own football team. The girls include Barbara McQuilliam, Wendy Hanson, Marjorie Mathews, Wendy Cross, Rita Miles, Marjorie Davies, Pam Greenaway, Kerry Holder, ? Gittins, Margaret Williams, Betty Lewis, Lindsay Price and Margoe Beddoe.

189. June 1953 saw the coronation of Queen Elizabeth II and here is a scene from the Hengoed Carnival that was held to help celebrate. The venue is the top field with a rare view of Hengoed Hall Farm which was demolished in the 1960s. Carnival Queen was Betty Hutchings and Flag Boy David Male. Many more names are given as Ivor, Blodwyn and Reg Male, Margaret Ellis, Megan Jenkins, Tommy Jenkins, Stewart Price, Elaine Ireland, Margaret Darcy, Doreen West, Sheila Stemp, Janet Randall, Jean Roberts, Phyllis Morgan, Grace Williams, Rona Evans, Iris Lewis, Wendy Lewis, Nina Powell, Gloria Powell, Margaret Ellis, Mr. Smart and Mrs.W. Dainton.

190. Members of Ystrad Mynach Youth Club are suitably costumed for a Halloween Night and are seen in the sports hall during the 1980s. Not all of the children's names have been traced but they do include Sarah Harvey, Laura Joshie, Clare Griffiths, Kerriann Evans, Tracy Campbell, Sharon Campbell, Louise Johns, Elizabeth Grey, Sarah Parry, Angela Kitchin, Rhian Lewis and Hannah Joshie.

191. Members of the Cefn Hengoed branch of the St. John Ambulance Brigade are pictured here during the 1950s, the photograph having been taken in the village hall which is now the site of the Magnum Stores. Some of the gentlemen are Kenny Brownsword, Johnny Capper, Noel McQuilliam, Abel Jones, Mr. McQuilliam, George Davies, Mr. Skyrme, Herbie Ward and Joe Brownsword.

192. This time some of the younger members of the brigade can be seen in the 1950s at the hall with Donald Humphries, Colin Williams, Johnny Capper, Tony Davies, Michael Smiga, Ronnie Oliver, Stephen Crocker, Harry Lewis, Tony Humphries, Terry Whittle and Henry Smiga.

193./194. The 50th anniversary of the end of war in Europe was celebrated in style everywhere, particularly so at Maesycwmmer with the inspiration of Terry Cannon and Len Davies's acquisition of an army personnel carrier to further enhance the atmosphere. There is a long list of those who were involved including Len and Jean Davies, Terry and Ann Cannon, Janet and Tony, Mandy and Terrence, Joanne, Dale, Shaun, Lynette, Anthony, Dean, Gaynor, Mathew, Samantha, Carol, Caroline, Paul, Glen, Mrs. Baker and around the vehicle are Kathy Davies, Maureen, Val, Ann, Ralph James, Debbie Butts, Angela, Amy Morgan, Eileen Butts, Tracie Lundy, Zoe Alderson, Rachel Johns and Stacy Baker.

195. The Red Hot Pokers of Hengoed were formed in 1980 and have managed to establish themselves as one of the most consistent and well-respected bands currently playing around the U.K. Individual band-members have worked and toured with a number of well-known artists and bands, with John 'Ned' Edwards playing with Van Morrison and appearing on both of his last albums. The artistes here are Liam McCafferty, Colin Griffin, John Edwards, Benny Herbert and Lyn. Adrian Gerrett and Howard are in the guises of horse and chicken.

196. More talented local musicians appear in this picture from 1995 by way of Hengoed's 'Lemon Wednesday' and they are Roger Wilde (drums), Brian Dauncey (lead guitar), John Turner (vocalist), Jeff Edwards (guitar and backing vocals), and Roger Mackenzie (bass guitar). Well-known around the valleys for their entertainment and after a spell of absence, they re-formed as a group in 1995 'by popular demand'.

197. The 1945 peace celebration, a 'Carnival Wedding' is in progress here at Raglan Road, Hengoed as it appropriately makes its way towards the chapel. The wedding party consists of Arnold Lewis, Marlene Ellis, John Darcy, Betty Lewis, Joyce Preston, Marjorie Ireland and Garcey Williams.

198. One of the finest plays ever performed in Maesycwmmer was during the 1950s, with a production of Robin Hood. The outfits were splendidly made down to the finest detail. Named where possible are - Maureen Picket, Viska Wallach, Maeve McPhearson, Pamela Furmage, Freda Weeks, Jacqueline Gibbs, Mary Russell, Avril Morris, Christine Milton, Andrea Jonathon, Diane Lewis, Bernice Prosser, Jean Morgan. Anne Furmage, Lynne Rees, Pauline Price, Elaine McDougall, Lydia Francis, Olwen Cannon, Valerie Morris, Pat Williams, Caroline Arthur, Glenys Snook, Margaret Morris, Kay William, Gaynor Morgan.

199. The Royal Wedding of 'Charles and Diana' was acknowledged by a street party laid on by the residents of North Avenue, Chave Terrace and Provident Cottages, Maesycwmmer in July 1981 and in amongst it all are - Jill, Philip, Mark and Andrea James, Dolly Jones, Brian Jones, Mr. and Mrs. Nicholas, Graham, Ros, Karen and Neil Roberts, Roy and Clare Cannon, Nancy and Brian Eales, Henry and Dot Alford, Bessie Skelding, John and Pat Humphries, Mr. and Mrs. Edward and Jean Cook, Eddie and Sue Griffin, G. Harris, Marge Powell, Mandy Jones and Lynsey Clark.

200. Hengoed School 'Gypsies' in the 1950s on the lawn at Hengoed House and some names to look out for are - Mstr. Thomas, Philip Selwood, Dai ?, Michael Fay, Gaynor Phillips, Valerie Wilson, Gwyn Jones, Gaynor Fox, Nina Powell, Pat Fowler, Judith?, Pat Blunt, Susan Porter, Gwyneth Morgan, Rosemary Gerrett, Moira Garbett, Janice Preston, Margaret Ellis, Ann Webb, Maureen Piper, Diane Jenkins, Joyce Preston, Jane Jones, Wendy Lewis, Elaine Follet and Pat Paske.

201. On the right is Ron Drew of Hengoed when attending a reunion of veterans from the battle of Arnhem in the Netherlands. Ron joined the army in 1940, beginning training with gliders and was amongst the first to land and take the bridge at Syracuse in Sicily, the prelude to the assault on Italy. He was to become a sergeant and served in North Africa before being called upon to take part in the main European campaigns in 1944, one of which was the near-disastrous Arnhem offensive to be known as 'Operation Market Garden'. Landing his glider in the village of Wolpheze, he fought his way on to Oosterbeek Church where the last battle orders of Lt. Col. Lonsdale had been pinned to the door! Following fierce street fighting, Ron and his platoon took refuge in the cellar of a house which was surrounded by German troops for four days until the door was eventually kicked open and an object thrown in.

Thinking this to be a grenade, they immediately ran into a corner of the room only to discover it was nothing more than a house brick! By this time however a huge Tiger tank was on the scene and Ron and his comrades were taken prisoner, spending the remainder of the war at Stalag 12a Neubrandenburg.

202. Another local military man albeit from an earlier period of conflict was Goeff Stevens of Ystrad Mynach who was a bugler in the Royal Horse Artillery and is pictured here at the outbreak of the First World War in August 1914. In what was at the time described as 'the war to end all wars', he saw action in some of the most fierce battles of the war on the Somme in France and Ypres and Paschendaele in Belgium. He was a noted cornet player in the Penallta Silver Band during its day and one of the highlights of his career was being able to play at the Royal Albert Hall with the famous BBC dance band leader and broadcaster Henry Hall, himself spending time in the Royal Artillery in the trenches of 1914-1916.

203. W.O. Graham Morgan of Cefn Hengoed served in the Royal Artillery from 1968 until 1993. During the Falklands conflict of 1982, he was credited with shooting down the first Argentinian aircraft with a Rapier missile fired from a shoreline battery. Graham narrowly escaped the Bluff Cove tragedy, having been taken off HMS Sir Galahad only minutes before the attack that took the lives of fifty souls including 32 Welsh Guardsmen on June 8th of that year.

204. During World War Two Ystrad Fawr housed a department of the Ministry of Food used for storage of vital food supplies for South Wales and the West of England, it having moved from Cardiff due to air attack. The days here were long and hard in wartime and the girls in the picture are Edith Hall, Olwen Edwards, Dorothy Sutton, Beryl Jones, Eloise Evans and Joan Jenkins.

205. A soldier from the ascribed 'forgotten war' - that of more than three years of battle in faraway Korea. This is Bryn Williams of Cefn Hengoed who served there, and he and his wife Doreen will be remembered as prominent villagers for their dedication and hard work associated with St. Ann's Church.

206. To conclude this military section is a photograph of Alice Meyrick of Maesycwmmer who served in the WRAC from 1940 to 1946 and the Territorial Army until 1949 proving the importance of the female contibution in wartime. Following this Alice worked in the domestic service for a number of notables in the area until retirement in 1974 and celebrated her 90th birthday in a local residential home in 2003.

207. The pensioners of Cefn Hengoed are gathered and dressed in patriotic costumes for the celebration of the Queen's Golden Jubilee in 2002, an event that had been planned months ahead. Seen left to right are - Back: Phil Cartright, Shirley Capper, Gwyneth Ilderton, Mervyn and Rita Miles, Eluned Gilbert, Arthur Rogers, Margaret Arthur, Laura Hughes, Muriel McCarthy, Penry Mathews, Beryl Taylor, Ellis Taylor, Lilian Brown. Middle: June Davies, Dilla Williamson, Silvia Carroll, Eva Morris, Hilda McCarthy, Edna Davies, Cassie Bowers. Front: Janice Drayton, Joan Davies, Beryl Morgan and Megan Mathews.

208. A school play at Derwendeg, Christmas 1981 had a huge cast and many of the names have been identified as follows - Curt Price, Lydia Rapecki, Adrian Morgan, Jason Atkinson, Mark Carroll, Dean McCarthy, Denise Maine, David Clark, David Thomas, Brian Wilding, John Hobbs, Stephen Morris, Michelle Taylor, Claire Walker, Alun Colyer, Kelvin O'Brian, Gareth Evans, Peter Lancett, Lee Holloway, Lee Walters, Heidi Sloggett, Joanne Gardiner, David Jay, Jane Thomas, Siân Thomas, Jason Morris, Jebran Khan, Gareth Powell, Michael Greenslade, Marcus Fortune, Lee Clapham, Alan Bowden, Mark Phillips, Lee Costa, Norman Chapman, Tony Evans, Sean Smith, Russell Knight, Paul Whitcombe, David Blackwell, Darren Skinner, Dean Dollaway, Terry Hurley, Ronald Woods, Gary Powell, Gary Kibble and Greg Hobbs.

209. Some more celebrations have been photographed here at Raglan Road, Hengoed in the 1940s comprised mainly of youngsters outside Tabernacle Church. Some of the names are Dolly Roberts, Dave Thomas, Marilyn Dovey, Terry Powell, Marion Williams, John Hopkins, Trevor Whatley, Dorian Powell, Jean Roberts, Barbara Norris and Coreen Roberts.

210. Ystrad Mynach station is the venue for these members of the Townswomen's Guild as they prepare for an outing to the Festival of Britain in London in 1951. In amongst the crowd are - Mrs. Davies, Betty Tomkinson, Heulwen Roberts, Rachel Arscott, Mrs. Emlyn Lloyd, Mrs. Maloney, Gwyneth Price, Mrs. Fred Davies and Mrs. Martin.

211. The Majorettes Jazz Band of Ystrad Mynach were consistent at winning championships around the country, collecting a number of trophies on the way, a credit to their organizers Ken and Silvia Pritchard, with Cliff and Mavis Pritchard. Pictured during the 1980s are - Dale Powell, Kevin Price, Roger Mosley, Derrick Pritchard, Kay Pritchard, Karen Metcalfe, Debbie Wiltshire, Lynette Gardiner, Denise Maine, Angela Hughes, Cliff Pritchard, ? Roberts, Ian Dallimore, Kim Pritchard, Donna Maine, Fay Jones, Adele Davies, Julia Morgan, Jane Humphries, Debbie Lewis, Paula Pritchard, Susan Williams and Kenneth Pritchard.

212. A very popular trio from Cefn Hengoed consisted of Lolly Lewis, Peggy Lewis and Ceridwen Rogers pictured next to Vince Saville in the centre and outside the gates of H.M. Prison Cardiff. Their performance was overwhelmingly received by an audience of inmates whose only disappointment it was said, was that the girls were dressed in new style multi-coloured trousers instead of fashionable mini skirts which might have caused a riot. Not knowing what some of the lyrics in the girls' songs might mean to such a male population gave them some concerns, nevertheless, all went well for such an event. Also in this picture are Colin Williams, George White and Cllr. Alan Rogers.

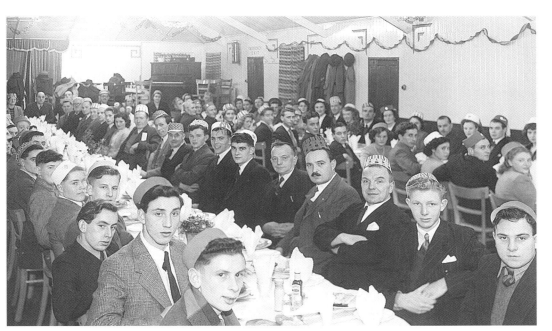

213. A scene from a Christmas party for the staff and families of Gywnn's Garage Ystrad Mynach that was held in the late 1950s in the Institute and a few faces have been traced such as - Bill Bampfield, David Thomas, Frank Batten, Graham Fewins, Don Branwen, Fred Campin, Colin Maloney, Gwyn Jones, Betty Jenkins, Jack Jenkins, Danny Ireland.

214. Former members of The Debonaires Jazz Band organized a reunion at the Cross Keys Inn, Cefn Hengoed in the year 2000 and here is a picture of those who attended - Jane McCarthy, Mary Young, Glynis Sellwood, Carol Sellwood, Yvonne Price, Teresa Williams, Tina Bragg, Madeline Roberts, Susan Price, Davina Oakley, Diane Jay, Susan Martin, Margaret Cullen, Marion Griffiths, Peggy Griffiths, Janet Wilding, Susie Griffiths, Tommy Price, Enid Price and Ken Griffiths.

215. The 40th anniversary of VE Day in 1985 provided another opportunity for the neighbours of Derwendeg Street, Cefn Hengoed to come out to party and amongst the very many are - Janine Hinder, Joanne Wilding, Joanne, Darren and Andrew Hegarty, Gemma Martin, Shaun Rogers, Liam Rogers, Evan Hellyar, Julie Dolloway, Lauren Williams, Katie Hellyar, Craig Vivian, Rhiannon Pitwood, Vicky Martin, Hannah Vivian, Joanne Hegarty, Alyn Rogers, Carol Hegarty, Marlene, Lee, Brenda and Dean Dolloway, Justin Hinder, Darren Meredith, Ellen Rogers, Glynis and Linda Sellwood, Christine Pitwood, Tina Norman, Lisa and Christine Meredith, Elaine Hellyar, Joy Rupnik, Keith Hellyar and Dale Tucker.

216. A grand turnout for an Easter bonnet parade in the 1970s at Maesycwmmer Senior Citizens Complex where unfortunately not all of the names have been discovered but in the group are - Back: Hannah Jones, Mrs. Watts, Mrs. Nicholas, Mrs. Case, unknown, unknown. Middle: unknown, unknown, Iris James, Rose Pickett, Mrs. Gardiner. Front: unknown, Marie Pritchard, Ron Case, Natalie Jones and Mr. Farr.

217. Cefn Hengoed Male Voice Choir are pictured outside the Cross Keys Inn with landlady Mrs. Hinwood in 1937 and the members are - Back: Arthur Price, Glyn Williams, Mr. Perrott, Mr. Morgan. Middle: Mr. Lewis, Walter Griffiths, David Williams, Ernie James, Constable Harry, Pat O'Connor, Cliff Pritchard, Owen Roberts, Cled Williams. Front: Harry Lewis, Hopkin Lewis, Mr. Burton, Mrs. Hinwood, Ron Hinwood, Tudor Price, William Price and Bryn James.

218. Council Chairman Hopkin Lewis oversees the first children's choir in the early 1960s, comprising of - Back: Sheila Williams, Marlene Bullock, Mionia James, Diane Thomas, Gwen Jones, Anne Long, Gaynor Wilkinson, Susan Jones, Margaret Young, Janice Griffiths. Row 3: Pam Williams, Lavinia Dalton, Eynon Roberts, Denise Bower, Susan Thomas, Alison Tucker, Valerie Young, ?. Row 2: Mrs. Winnie Williams, Mrs. Blanche Jones, Megan Williams, Julie Vaughan, Eileen James, Sheila Poulton, Julie Taylor, Hillary De La Taste, M. Sharp, Rose Morris, Christine Roberts, Marlene Jones, Christine Price, ?, Dorothy Cutliffe, Cled Williams. Front: Carol Lewis, Pat Roberts, ? Tipper, ? Israel, Mr. Sheen (Conductor), Mrs. Peggy Lewis, Hopkin Lewis, Maureen Corbin (Pianist), Pauline Roberts, Wendy Tyler, Vanessa Jones, Janice Cushion, Lynda Saunders and Rosemary Cutliffe.

219. The organisers of the VE Celebrations 1985 who helped to make such a memorable day for all are pictured here in Bethel Chapel. Carol Kibble, Cherrie Clapham, Lillian Collier, Lillian Stacey, Pat Griffiths, Mary Griffiths, Enid Watkins, Beryl Bolter. Sarah O'Conner, Betty O'Conner, Barbara Hall nursing Joanne Beynon, Janet Beynon, Dilys Thomas, Gillian Arnold, Rowena Withshire, Yvonne Davies, Marilyn Whitcombe and Peggy Holton.

220. Hop-picking used to be a popular seasonal occupation for many years ago, as witnessed in this 1930s photograph from West Hope Farm, Hereford that includes Harriet Lewis, Doreen Ellis and Cliff Ireland. Fleets of lorries would be seen loaded with all the necessities for a couple of weeks stay in the temporary huts provided for the pickers and after a hard day's work, much fun would be had around the camp fires. The only problem was concern by the authorities for families taking their children along too, and if reported for missing school, an appearance at Bargoed Court and a £1 fine awaited their return!

CHAPTER 9

Then and Now

221./222. A Pontypool-bound train approaches the Maesycwmmer side of the viaduct after leaving Hengoed High Level station on a frosty morning during the early 1960s. The lower part of Hengoed can be seen through the smoke and fog in this photograph of the Vale of Neath railway line. The lower picture shows the viaduct as it is today, the railway line having been replaced by a cycle track and walkway and with it being opened to the public, an excellent opportunity has been provided to illustrate the views that were available during the days of rail travel. In the picture are Alf Thomas, Elaine Jones, Karen Roberts, Ros Roberts, Marion George and Grant Stevens.

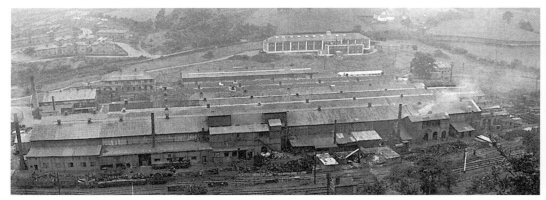

Powell Duffryn Associated Collieries Limited

223./224. This 1949 panoramic view of Tredomen engineering works was taken from the rock formation that towers above the factory and shows the full 16.3 acre site of the works that was once a major employer. Providing more than 650 jobs, Tredomen Works was built by the Powell Duffryn Company in 1922 to manufacture and supply mining machinery for their numerous pits. The National Coal Board took control in 1950 and with the run-down of the coal industry and consequently the services of the works, the site was cleared and the area has now been redeveloped into an attractive business park. The former NCB computer centre seen at the top of the photograph is now occupied by Caerphilly County Borough Museums and Heritage. The village of Tredomen can be seen top left on both photographs and in the foreground the brand new Tredomen Business Park can be seen. The new centre brings together the main local business support agencies to provide a more focused and complete support service for local firms. The centre also houses a fully integrated training facility in association with The College Ystrad Mynach.

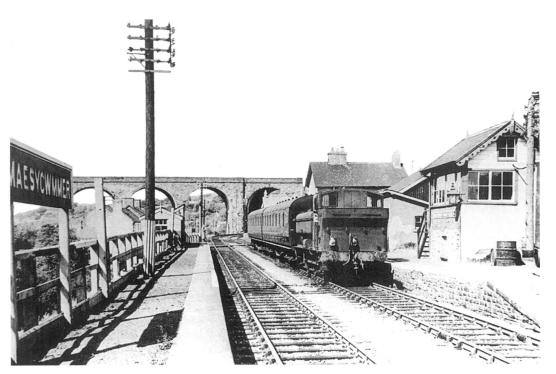

225./226. Two views taken from the same spot, facing north in the direction of the viaduct. Maesycwmmer station with the Brecon and Merthyr line can be seen in the top picture with a passenger train at the down platform waiting to travel on to Bedwas and thence Newport. The modern-day photograph below presents a much-changed scene showing the Maesycwmmer Inn and The Butcher's Arms from where a platform would have been, all part of the redevelopment completed in the 1970s.

227./228. The lower part of King's Hill can be seen in these two photographs. The houses in the foreground of the modern picture are now three-storey buildings and thus obstruct the view of the Junction Inn. Owner and builder Mr. Percy Briggs is restoring Glamorgan House to its former self after studying old photographs of the area as it looked before the arrival of the nearby shops and houses in years gone by.

229./230. The top photograph shows the once-familiar buckets of slag and waste on their way to the giant tips that were a common sight in the coalmining days. The power house, shafts and two stacks can be seen in the background and the bottom scene is the picture today, with only the two shafts and power house standing derelict awaiting the proposed development of modern housing. The former colliery was the last working pit in the Rhymney Valley and despite all the efforts to preserve it and the valuable jobs, it finally closed on November 1st 1991.

231./232. The two views seen here of Penallta Road in Ystrad Mynach were taken almost fifty years apart. The well-known name of Boots the chemist with Shakespeare's jewellers next door may be remembered and the Co-op butchery which is now Shirley Fabrics. On the right was Matthews the popular building supplier which has since been replaced by the local Spar shop.

233./234. When the first of these two pictures was taken, the Coopers Arms was just an isolated alehouse nestling in the lower end of Ystrad Mynach where there were a few other scattered dwellings such as the forge mill and the elegant Ystrad Fawr. Above, the landlord and his family pose with a few visiting patrons who may well have been members of the Lindsay household of Ystrad Fawr judging by the horse and carriage at their disposal. Below, this is the inn as it stands in the twenty-first century, surrounded by extensions to the college and the building of a housing estate.

235./236. Bedwlwyn Road is the setting for these two contrasting views where the building belonging to Barclays Bank provides a major change to the scene. The Beech Tree Hotel is at the top of the road and apart from G.W. Jones the florist, many of the older established names such as Bracchi, Fines etc. have now gone. Once prominent farmers, the family of florist owners Graham Jones now hail as the longest-running family business in the area.

237./238. A view looking towards Ystrad Mynach taken from the viaduct during the 1950s. The open fields to the right of the picture were to become the Avenue running alongside the new road that was built in the early 1920s and below is the scene as it appears eighty years later.

Acknowledgements

The authors wish to express their sincere thanks to the undermentioned who kindly loaned photographs and information used in the compilation of this book.

Adrian Barwood, Mrs. Beddoe, Mrs. Beer, Dai Beynon, Alan Biggs, Ray Bishop, Cassie Bowers, Gaynor Boulton, Michelle Brideaux, Mervyn Burtch MBE, Caerphilly County Borough Museum and Heritage, Cefn Hengoed OAP, John Collins, Lillian Colyer, Ken Cross, Mrs. D. Dally, Gareth Davies, Len and Jean Davies, Ron and Henry Drew, Ann Edmunds, Jeff and Ned Edwards, John Edwards, Robert Evans, Trevor Everson, Bob Fordham, Chris Griffin, Kath Griffiths, Mike Guilfoyle, Marion Gurner, Nancy Gurner, Lindsey Gwynn, Alan Hayter, Tom Hayward, Brian Heffron, Peter Hegarty, Mrs. Holder, Paul James, Jill James, Joan Jenkins, Jills Corner Shop, Dorothy John, Gren Jones M.B.E., Hector Jones, Susan Lacey, Lolly and Peggy Lewis, The Lindsay Club, Mrs. Judith Matthews, Terry Matthews, Phil McDougall, Ellien Meara, Alice Meyrick, Alan Morgan, Mrs. B. Morgan, Christene Morgan, Graham Morgan, Mrs. Mullins, Bernard Murphy, Dr. Sue Noake (Lewis Girls Comprehensive School), William Norman, Lynda Osborne, Mr. and Mrs. Packer, Idris Penrose, Maureen Pickett, Giuseppe Platoni, Susan Price, Cliff and Mavis Pritchard, Mrs. Margaret Pritchard, Mrs. Betty Rees, Hywell Roberts, Roslyn Roberts, Terry Roberts, Dino Spinetti, Grant Stevens, Dave and Pat Thomas, Gethin Thomas, Judith Voyle, Ken Walker, Mrs. Ward, Trevor Whatley, Mrs. Ann Williams, Bryn Williams, Gary and Margaret Williams, Lynn Williams, Michael Williams, Mike Williams, Minnie Williams, Nia Williams, Ystrad Mynach Hospital, Ystrad Mynach and Bargoed Libraries, Ystrad Mynach Bowls Club.

Also available by the same authors:

Old Ystrad Mynach
including Hengoed,
Cefn Hengoed and Maesycwmmer
in Photographs
- Volume 1

ISBN 1 874538 39 5

Old Gelligaer
including Pen-y-bryn, Pen-pedair-heol,
Cascade and Glyn-gaer
in Photographs
- Volume 1

ISBN 1 874538 79 4

**Available from bookshops or direct from
Old Bakehouse Publications
Tel: 01495 212600 Fax: 01495 216222
email: oldbakehouseprint.co.uk**